THE IMPROV MINDSET

How to Make Improvisation
Your Superpower for Success

KEITH SALTOJANES

For Amanda.
The one person who believed in me.
Sometimes all we need is just one.

TABLE OF CONTENTS

PREFACE

Before I started my journey into learning improv (or improvisation as nerds like me call it), I was incredibly shy. One could even say the shyest of shy. And one did say that...me, just now. But I wasn't always that way.

When I was younger, I would perform skits[1] for relatives on different holidays, getting into character by wearing costumes I made out of paper and crayons. In preschool, I would dress like a different animal each day to go to school, wearing more costumes built with paper (back then, killing lots of trees for comedy wasn't thought twice about). Later, I even made a makeshift stage in my basement and would entertain/torture my family and neighbors by making them enjoy/endure my variety revues, which were just me doing bad impressions or characters lip-syncs.

But then, with a mixed society, bullying (who was to know I'd get bullied for dressing in a paper dog costume?), and school teachers telling me to sit down, be quiet, and stop being creative...

I shut down. Became a shell of my creative self with no personality or difference between me and a piece of furniture.

Cut to years later, and I discovered improv, and more than 20 improv years later, I'm still doing it.[2]

It might sound cliché, but improv changed my life. I went from being that shy kid who never said anything, and was only talked to by a very small

---

[1] Skits are what children do at summer camp. Sketches are what adults do and are written and rehearsed. Scenes are what we do in improv. Please don't call those skits.

[2] Improv years are like regular years, but with more bits...and keep reading to learn about bits.

triangle of friends – a triangle because there wasn't even enough to make a circle - to not being able to not use improv with every human interaction in my everyday life. I gained lifelong friendships, have gotten jobs (both in my field and not), and became the creative kid I was when I was little, but with all the knowledge, experience, and freedom that comes with being an adult.

Although this book is not my life story or even my comedy story, it's all part of our story, which includes your story – get it? No matter how much we learn or put these improv skills to use, we can always get better. Improv is an ever-evolving skillset. We can get better at it, but we can always learn more because, at the end of the day – it's still just making stuff up in the moment.

Hopefully, this book will either:

a) Help you use these skills of improv to better your own life
b) Learn some new skills, whether you've taken an improv class before or are as new as they come (we've all been there).
c) Give you the start into your own journey with improv, and lead to you doing more classes and even shows
d) Inspire you to make paper costumes (maybe not)

No matter the reason, remember that you don't have to be born witty and charming to be good at improv. Anyone can do it. Literally *anyone*. You just have to step outside your comfort zone.

So read on and learn, and while the only way to really get better at improv, or anything for that matter, is to get up and do it and fail, and do it again, and not fail, and again and fail, and again and again and again until you fail less... this book is a good place to start.

INTRODUCTION

Hold on a second... if the only way to learn improv is by getting up and doing it, then why are you sitting in that chair, lying on your bed, or reading this on a plane from a PDF you stole from the internet? Because improv is a skill just like driving a car, learning to cook, or figuring out how the new update on your phone works...and there are methods to it that we can study and learn to then apply to the actions of doing it and getting better along the expedition.

With that said, there are a few ways you can use this book to learn:

a) Read it from start to finish as words on a page, and that's all.
b) Open to random pages to do exercises as needed.
c) Use it for display on a shelf to show people you know what improv is.
d) Take your time and do the exercises as they are laid out in each chapter, and put them to practice every day until they become a habit.

Now that first way will give knowledge to your brain and allow you to talk about what you've learned, but putting it into action is going to be difficult, and you'll more than likely fall back into your old ways of dealing with stressful moments.

The second way can work if you've studied improv for some time and are just looking for quick hits of inspiration.

The third way was mostly a joke, but I guess you could really do that.

But the fourth way is the most effective. Learning any new skill is about the experience of doing it, and to squeeze the most out of this "training guide" is to treat it as a class, which means do the work - remember those classes in school we just slid by in, showing up only for attendance sake and doing the bare-minimum so we can pass? Yeah, don't do that here; it'd be a waste! The exercises in this book offer to expand your experiences outside of just reading words, and to engage with the world around you more creatively to build your confidence and creativity. Plus, there's no final grade, except for how much you put into it. Some people think because improv is "made up" there's nothing to learn. That if you aren't naturally hilarious, you can't do it. That's untrue. Did you not read the preface? The word 'pre' is in it because it's supposed to come first. Come on! But if you didn't, here's a summary- anyone can learn this with the right guidance, and that's what I'm going to try to do through these words I wrote months/years/centuries ago from my computer.[3]

This book is focused on how to use improv in our everyday life, and you may never have a goal of performing improv or acting – and that's perfectly fine. However, we will use the tools of improv here, which sometimes are best demonstrated through acting exercises and improvised scenework. But trust me, if you can do an improvised scene, knowing nothing at all before you start, having to go into a conversation, presentation, or social situation with some knowledge ahead of time – such as the people there, subject, etc. - you will be that much better equipped to handle those non-performance activities. So while learning exercises that seem indirectly related to our lives, the skills created in our brain will be directly able to be put to use in life. Again, you'll have to trust me.

Everything I teach is a combination of everything I've learned from everyone and everywhere; my teachers, my mentors, in improv, acting, comedy,

---

[3] Depending on when you are reading this. How's the future?

travel, relationships, life, and more. I've taken it all and put it into one distilled-focused study. Sláinte!

While I feel that most of the schools of improv I learned from taught reactionary improv classes- as in, you get on stage and do the exercise, things go wrong, and the instructors tell you how to fix it, but usually never why something worked when it does- the style I found works best is proactive- which means we can explain the exercise, its goal, and you can do it and learn how and why you did certain things during it, what worked and didn't all without having to ever step foot into a group improv class setting.

As I said earlier, you can never master improv, and even now, at the 20+ year mark, I'm still making mind-opening discoveries. It does take time and as they say, to be an expert at anything takes 10,000 hours.[4] You'll still have to put your time in, read, study, think, test the concepts out in the real world, fail, and get up and do it again. But my goal is to shave some of that frustrating time off for you.

Since improvisation is an ever-evolving, new-ish artform, the things I'm saying here are not the end all and be all of improv (if you hear a teacher suggest that, then that's a red flag in my opinion). I aim to use these lessons to further your understanding of how improv works and loosen up the tangled over-thinking thoughts life has created in our brains. The more you try out the lessons in this book, the more you may find paths that work better for you inspired by what you read. That's great! That's how things evolve. So learn, get better, and get inspired and let's go.

---

[4] See the 10,000-Hour Rule in *Outliers* by Malcolm Gladwell (but only after finishing this book, OK?)

FIRST EXERCISE: You Are Amazing:

By reading this book and doing the exercises within, we will hopefully expand upon your unique life. But before we get any further, we want to set a foundation that you have already done some amazing things up to this point.

IMPROV EXERCISE

YOU ARE AMAZING

How to Do It:

01 Write down 5 things you have done that you are proud of.

02 After you have them down, put them somewhere where you can look at them every morning to start your day with the reminder of how badass you actually are.

These 5 things could be anything from a goal you once accomplished, to a personal thing, or someone you have in your life...it doesn't matter. All that matters is that it's something that you have a positive memory of. Even if you don't feel like it right now, you accomplished these things big in your life, so it's a good reminder that you are more powerful than you may think you are.

SECOND EXERCISE: Goals

There's power to writing things down and getting them out of our busy minds filled with other thoughts. So as simple as this exercise seems, it can have vast results.

GOALS: PART 1

How to Do It:

1 Write down 5 things you want or goals you'd like to achieve. This could be anything big or small, but something you desire.

2 Once completed, put your list away someplace; no need to revisit them for the time being.

For these two exercises, you can start an improv journal, or use sticky notes, or a note taking app...whatever works for you, as long as you actually do it – no matter how silly you think they may be.

Done? Okay, let's carry on.

CHAPTER 1

HOW TO IMPROVISE

Wait, really? No more backstory? Are we really going to start learning now? Yes, *and* all that was part of the learning, jerk.[5]

What is Improv?

First of all, what even is improv!? Is it what Jerry Seinfeld does? Or Maybe it's a TV show like *The Office*. OR maybe it's the word *improve,* but I've been spelling it wrong?

Nope, no, wrongzo. Improv means to be in a situation or scenario without anything pre-planned and fully reacting in that moment without knowing what we will say beforehand. In an improv performance done by improv actors, this takes the form of an improv show on a stage in front of an audience, but also we experience these same moments every day in life, which is basically a 24 hour improv show in itself (unless someone gives us a script of what to do and say at every moment in our day, and if so, good for you Mr./Mrs. President).

What Jerry Seinfeld does is standup comedy, which is reciting a tirelessly thought-about, written down, edited, memorized, and practiced act to make it look like it's happening in the moment. Likewise, fully scripted and memorized shows like *The Office* are filmed to resemble a documentary, which are not scripted, but are indeed not improvised. Even shows like *Curb Your Enthusiasm*, which is known as an improvised show, only is so

---

[5] The real jerk is the person who wrote that…wait, that's me!

through dialogue. Before going into the scenes, the actors know the pre-written outline of what should happen in the scene itself, and they can make up the words in the moment - so still not fully improvised. And as much as my spell check thinks I mean *improve* when I wrote *improv*, they are also very different from each other.

When we wake up and go about our day, we mostly have an idea of what's going to happen – if we're going to the grocery store or work, we will base our assumptions on the possible future experiences of what happened in the time previously at those places. We get most nervous in new situations because we have no prior memories of them, and thus, it's the unknown - even though our mind tries to connect it to something familiar to make us feel safer (like when we think, "oh, this person reminds me a bit of someone else I know."). Even in familiar situations like work or the store, it's when something different than our preconception the day happens that catches us off guard, and we freeze and don't know what to say – now we're in the improv territory!

What is an "Improv Mindset?"

Improvisers have learned these skills to better their craft of acting, writing, or even just performing improv shows. Off-stage they are quick-witted humans who find the fun in everyday life. They don't overthink everything they say and, at best, live in the moment and find the positive in every idea. We can literally say or do anything we want in improv, and training our mind to that, too, will allow us to respond quicker in any situation

Even if you never want to step on a stage, in front of a camera, or do anything creative outside of getting better at what you do in your life now, improv still is beneficial.

Maybe it's an upcoming speech at a friend's wedding, or giving a presentation at work, or just talking to your work boss to get a raise, or maybe you want to network better at parties, or just talk *at all* at parties (I've been there), or a first date, or talking to a barista when you get a coffee, or when a stranger stops and asks direction, or, or, or ...the circumstance in which we don't know what exactly is going to happen in our lives is endless.

So whether you are starting a journey onto becoming an improv comedian or not, learning to have an "Improv Mindset" – one that has freedom, creativity, and confidence to live fully in any moment, will greatly help you whenever such improv scenarios come your way.

Let Go

So with all of that, the first step in learning "how to improvise' is to let go of trying to control every moment around us. Stop thinking so much and judging everything that pops into our heads before it even has a chance to come out of our mouths.

As stated before (see, there were reasons for those first two sections), when we were children, we would all say whatever and do whatever we felt like. But then we became trained to live in society by adults around us. The thing is, this training was learned by them based on their own parent's training and/or on fears of being judged and out-of-date prehistoric human survival instincts (i.e., if we don't act like everyone else, the tribe will leave us and we'll have to survive in the wilderness alone and surely perish). There's no blame to be given here; they were only doing the best they could with what they learned. But it's our responsibility to now break this pattern passed on since our cave days.

Thus, we learned to overthink *everything* we say and do. This, of course, can be a good thing in our world because if we did and said whatever we wanted all the time, a number of negative things could hurt other people emotionally and ourselves, probably physically. But also, maybe some positive things could happen that'd we'd never know about...the unknown is ripe for opportunity.

Stop Judging

So within that step of letting go, we must also stop judging ourselves. Stop judging others, too, while you're at it. Just stop judging![6] Your mind is telling you what to do and say in every moment, but then our ego/fear/parent's voice is censoring and judging everything between our brain and our mouth, and we freeze up. It's time to ignore that ego/fear/parent's voice and let your mind and instincts get back to work. Most of us were brought up this way so forgive yourself (and anyone else) that has stifled your creativity. Again, stop judging- even that.

I have a saying/rule/repeated mantra that comes up in classes: *There is no wrong answer except no answer.* Say it with me: *There is no wrong answer, except no answer.*

Good.

If there is no wrong answer, then the flip side of that also means that every answer is right! The only wrong answer is no answer.[7]

Instead of standing there thinking about what to say, trying to be witty or funny or thinking what someone else would say in this situation and judging how all our ideas are dumb, say *anything*. Once it's out of our mouth, then we just expand on it more to make sense of it afterwards, which is easier than responding with that first sentence. The hard part is over! But...I'm jumping ahead so more on this later, I swear.

---

[6] Unless you are a courtroom Judge, then by all means judge away!

[7] But please don't use this as a reason to be offensive

Now, since most people are constantly judging what they say, it is difficult to say whatever comes into our mind without a long delay. That's OK, because when learning improv, there will be a learning curve, and we should try to make mistakes during that curve. Mistakes mean we are trying. We can't be perfect yet, so just *go for it*. If you fall on your face (literally or figuratively), then you learned something for next time and will be that much better. Instead of trying to think of the most creative and best ideas when doing these exercises, just go with the very first thing that pops into your head. We normally already pick-and-choose what we think is better, so here let's do it differently and stop that pre-judgment in our heads.

Exercises

Ok, so we understand we have to let go and stop judging, but how do we do it? With improv exercises. This book is filled with exercises you can do to get into the present moment, let go of stress, think quicker, and strengthen your overall "Improv Mindset" - which brings us to our first exercises. You can do these now or whenever you have to do something in life or work that requires you to use your quick brain-thinking.

EXERCISE: Shake and Stretch

Creativity is best done not only by our thinking mind but also by our whole body. We want to re-train ourselves to live not only as let-me-think-hard-about-that creatures, overthinking everything in our heads- but to be within our entire selves. That's what this exercise assists with.

This exercise can be done in the privacy of a bathroom, at home before you leave, outside before you go into a place, or even in the lobby (just do it smaller), before a meeting, presentation, or anything else you may feel anxious about.

SHAKE & STRETCH

SKILLS USED: Being Present + Stress Relief + Loosening Up Body

1 ## HOW TO DO IT
Stand up and literally shake it all out - shake your arms, your legs, your neck (carefully), your hands, do some small, quiet, jumps...shake everything. This will put you in your body as we get present with the feeling of our entire body and limbs getting a rush of blood sent to it.

2 ## STRETCH IT OUT
Slowly bend at your waist and let yourself hang with your arms loose; you don't have to touch your toes, just hang. Let out any sounds or noises you feel within you with an audible *sigh*.

3 ## TAKE A DEEP BREATH
...in, hold it for a moment, and then release. Repeat that 4-8 times.

4 ## SLOWLY
...one vertebra at a time, stand back up to resting position. At the top, take another deep breath in and let it out.

5 ## FULLY NOTICE
...the space and sounds around you in this present moment. You may feel light headed from the extra oxygen or moving your body, but that's normal as you probably aren't used to doing this exercise.

GOAL: feel more relaxed & present - ready to face whatever is coming your way.

EXERCISE: Word Association

Don't worry, this isn't a psychological exam looking at the words you say as having meaning ("oh, you said *ice cream* after the word *beach* – that must mean your parents never loved you when you were younger... nothing like that). It's all about letting your mind connect to the last thing you heard and not judging or overthinking.

Creativity doesn't come from randomness. It comes from being inspired by something we experience with our senses. So for this exercise, we'll be inspired by a word we hear.

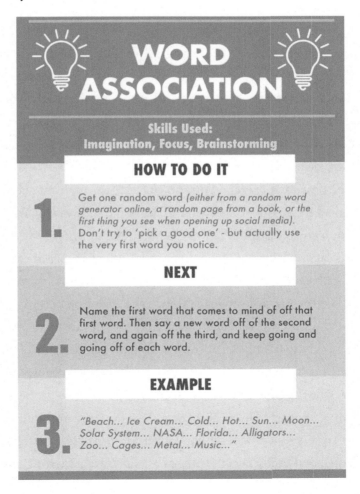

The **goal** here is to show you that you have ideas in your head if you get out of your own way and allow your mind to connect to them, and by doing so, you will never run out of stuff to say or think of. Every new idea is inspired by something that came before it.

As in the example, see how we got to the word *Music* from starting with *Beach*. Now those two things aren't directly related to each other, and there's no way someone would first think of the topic of *Music* when they hear the word *Beach*, but connecting words to each other leads us to new ideas. Easy right?

Tips:

- Don't judge yourself or try to think of the "right word" each time. Remember, there is no wrong answer except for no answer, so keep doing it, and you'll get faster and can go further each time.
- All the words shouldn't relate to the first word. That first word is only the jumping off point that can bring many other unrelated ideas down the line.
- This is a great exercise you can practice throughout the day. Try it next time you are stuck in traffic, bored in a waiting room, or in a dull conversation (...ok maybe not the last one).
- It's easy to "cheat" at this game, and think of a word ahead of time. But that defeats the purpose. You should really only be reacting off of the previous word said, not the even one before it, but the most recent word. You can tell if you're cheating by a word not connecting (using the above example, when the word is *Sun* and you say *Chocolate*. Those don't really relate because you went back to the previous word, *Ice Cream*.)
- You can repeat words already said, or even say opinions (so if the word was *Ice Cream*, replying with *My favorite* is perfectly fine.
- You can literally say anything at all. There is no wrong answer!

Advanced Version:

There are a few ways you can push yourself to get even better at Word Association. One way is to use a timer. Set it for 30 seconds to start, and keep going to say as many words as you can within that time without stopping. Then do it again for longer and again for longer. See how long you can go before your mind starts to judge yourself and you stop thinking as quickly.

Another way is to teach a friend the game and play it with them, going back and forth as fast as possible, without long delays between each answer. You have no idea what they will say next, so it will work on improvising in the moment!

When you are really ready to put this concept to the test, use Word Association when in conversation with someone. For example, if they mention the beach, you could always follow-up with a memory of how you used to eat ice cream after going to the beach and if they ever had a tradition like that. It's all just using and building upon what came before.

These exercises may seem simple, but they are indeed powerful to help us start to get our minds in that of an improviser, and the more we practice them, the better we'll get at using those skills.

Who Can Be Good at Improv?

Everyone.

But REALLY, Even I Can Be Good at Improv?

Anyone and everyone, and that includes you. A lot of people think they can't do improv because they don't think they are funny, witty, quick, creative, or just plain aren't brave enough. All of those are lies you're telling yourself. Sure, maybe already being one or more of those things will give you a slightly better head start when learning improv, but it shouldn't stop you.

I've said it a lot already and I'll say it again - literally *anyone* can improvise and be really good at it! I bet at least one of you is thinking "Yeah, well, not me, I'm different. I can't learn it."

Lies!

I've taught thousands of students from all walks of life, parts of the world, careers, and personalities and *every single one of them* came into class the first day, a little nervous and not sure what to do but went on stage a few weeks later and were able to not only respond, in the moment, but also perform a successful improvised scene. So when I say anyone can learn it, I truly mean anyone. We learned that improv is a skill, and like any other skills, can be taught and learned, even by you.

But I'm Not Funny

Let's just squash this right here and now - nowhere in the definition of the word "improv" does it say anything about being funny; it just has to be made up without any preconceived ideas. A lot of times, it's assumed we have to be funny since most people associate improv with comedy. The most well-known example of modern improv is the show *Whose Line Is It Anyway,* and they aim to be comedic improv. They're doing a style known as short-form improv and are purposely doing a comedy show to get viewers, that's why that exists. But improv itself doesn't always have to be funny.

There are styles and forms of improv performance that purposely don't try to be funny and focus more on dramatic storytelling. They use all the same skills as comedic improv, just stay more grounded and focus on more serious subjects. And since we are focusing here more on using improv skills in life, and not for performance – if non-comedic improv can exist within the world of improv performance, then surely it can exist in using these abilities in life.

However, improv *usually* turns out funny since we are making things up and the combination of ideas and minds, when put on the spot, come out humorously. And if you are reading this book to learn to be funny, it will also help you with that in the coming chapters, yes, but stop putting pressure on yourself *trying* to be funny.

Nothing is less funny than someone trying to be witty or funny. People can tell you're trying, and it's just plain uncomfortable. If you want to only be funny and nothing else, then look into sketch comedy or standup, where you can control the situation by writing it out and rehearsing it before ever showing it to anyone (not what improv is).

Real laughter comes from creating unexpected words, situations, and connections that happen in the moment – the "you had to be there" experience. By being truthful to whatever the situation is mixed with your personality, comedy will come from that, not one-liners and pop-culture references. But again, you do not have to be funny!

What Stops You

So, if you don't *have* to be funny, what else stops people from thinking they can't be good at improv? It may be one reason you are reading this book in the first place. This is a concept that I got from one of the best improv teachers *and* performers around, Susan Messing.[8] Besides being a fantastic teacher and dynamic performer is her fearlessness on stage, which may be evident in the following quote:

Susan says, "You're only limited by your lack of imagination and fear of appearing stupid...the worst thing that happens if you look stupid is that people might laugh at you, and we're doing comedy, so fuck you."

For improvisers, to be afraid of looking stupid, when, again, improv usually leans towards being funny, is a waste of time. We get to play and pretend to be someone else on stage, so letting that stop goes against everything you should be doing when improvising.

But, this concept also very much applies to our lives too.

1) Lack of Imagination

Some people think that they aren't _____ enough. This could be any adjective you want: creative, funny, smart, interesting, witty, born-with-it, etc. But that's just not true.

What improv teaches us is that every experience we've ever had can be pulled from to fuel our imagination, and by not self-judging, we can access those things that truly make us unlike anyone else. Having a lack of imagination isn't what stops us. It's *thinking* we have a lack of imagination.

Unless you live in a box and this book was given to you through the small opening that you breathe through, you have an expansive imagination to pull from because you have life experiences. Every moment of your life, big or small, significant or boring, leading up to this moment right now

---

[8] Susan is a founding member of The Annoyance Theater in Chicago, as well as an influential teacher for her work at Second City and iO theaters. If you ever get a chance to study with her or watch her perform- DO IT.

has filled your brain with memories, references, pictures, and emotions – and it's accessing and combining those memories that give anyone the ability to be creative. The best part, no one else in the entire universe has the same mixture of experiences as you.

Everything that we've done and encountered in our life – either in real life or have seen in movies or online or in books, etc.- can feed our "improviser's mind." The best part about this is no one can be as creative as you because you have something that no one else has, your *own* life experiences. But we get in our own way by comparing ourselves to others thinking we aren't enough, and before we can even get going, we stop any forward momentum of creative thinking. Your greatest superpower lies within your own experiences, tastes, and memories, so be proud of them! You have an entire life's worth of experience.

For example, the person who would have had the most crossover of my own life experiences would be my younger sister. We grew up in the same town, in the same house, with the same parents, celebrated the same holidays, went to the same school, etc. Yet we are still *very* different from each other. She lives on the East Coast, has kids, works in an office, and likes baking cupcakes. I am none of those things...even though we have the same past! So no one, not even a close relative, has the same experiences as you, and no one has those specific memories to pull from except you.

When we are communicating or trying to be creative, we often think that our experiences aren't good enough and have to come up with something new. But why waste energy doing that when we can just use what's in our brains already? For example, I'm going to describe two houses:

1) It's grey, one story, and has bushes in the front that are overgrown.
2) It's yellow, two stories, and has a fenced in yard.

Now, which of these houses do you think I actually lived in in my actual life? No way to be sure, huh? It's the second one. I lived there for 12 years and can easily describe many parts of that house in detail. The first one, my brain had to do more work and combine elements of other houses I've seen to create a new image. But guess what? The result from someone who is looking at what I said from the outside is the same. You didn't know if I lived in one, both, or lived in neither! But for me, one was much easier to create in my mind- the one I knew.

Use what you know because no one else can do it like you can. You are the only person who can do that, so don't think it's not enough. For all we know, you made it up anyway, it just takes less thinking. Why go through all the trouble of coming up with something new, when you can just use what you know? You are enough.

You can practice accessing all your ideas in your mind with an exercise called Zoomies[9]

---

[9] Every improv game and form has a random name picked in the moment. This concept was given two names by students so it has both and neither. Enjoy!

EXERCISE: Zoomies

This is similar to *Word Association* but in a direct, visual way. The exercise shows us that we can never run out of ideas if we use our experiences.

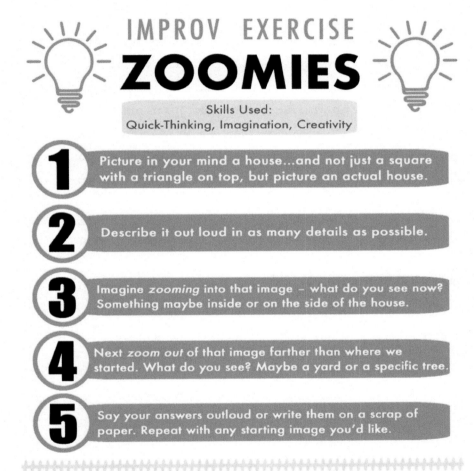

IMPROV EXERCISE

ZOOMIES

Skills Used:
Quick-Thinking, Imagination, Creativity

1 Picture in your mind a house...and not just a square with a triangle on top, but picture an actual house.

2 Describe it out loud in as many details as possible.

3 Imagine *zooming* into that image – what do you see now? Something maybe inside or on the side of the house.

4 Next *zoom out* of that image farther than where we started. What do you see? Maybe a yard or a specific tree.

5 Say your answers outloud or write them on a scrap of paper. Repeat with any starting image you'd like.

All I said in that example was to picture a house, and after some 'zooming' we can get three images from that. Now I'm willing to guess that all the things you described are things you've experienced in your real life. Maybe even you pictured the house you grew up in.

And if not your actual house, but one you made up, then it was a combination of pieces of things that you've actually also seen or experienced in either in real life, or in movies or TV. It all comes from your own experience. So by picturing the word you heard and then *zooming* in or out from that image, it will allow you to come up with more ideas.

So the **goal** here is to show you that you can't ever go blank, or run out of ideas, or "I don't know what to say or do" because it's all about allowing our mind to make the connections for us. The hardest thing to do in improv is to come up with the very first idea. It was much easier for you to picture a house when I said to "picture a house" compared to if I said "picture something" because the options are endless there. But starting with something tangible, like a house, can easily give us more ideas.

Try this for yourself by opening a book and pointing to a random word – and zooming in and out to create more images and ideas from that word.

2) Fear of Appearing Stupid

So if Lack of Imagination doesn't exist, then maybe the thing that holds us back is the fear of looking stupid or embarrassment.

When doing improv for an audience, it's very scary to step on stage and perform a show when we have no preconceived ideas of what we're going to do. The chances of being embarrassed and look stupid are enormous! But that's part of the fun of improv, and you'd be surprised how well you can do when you just throw yourself out there - and after you do it, you'll feel exhilarated!

Embarrassment is a real thing that most of us work our entire lives to get away from. Most people don't want to look stupid out of many fears that we have in our heads. But while that fear of embarrassment exists, the thing to do is not let it stop us. What's the worst that can happen? Everyone is all too busy in their lives for anyone to judge us as much as we think people are judging us or as much as we pre-judge ourselves. We're all human and make mistakes, and most people only laugh or judge because they are too afraid of something embarrassing happening to them. Can you imagine going through life without embarrassment? Well, at one point, we all did.

When we were kids, we weren't afraid of anything, until we were told that there was a risk of losing friends and possibly not fitting in (i.e., people will laugh at you or think less of you), then our heads filled us with so much fear that it froze us. But if we can get back into that playful mood and not take everything so seriously, it's the most powerful way to move past fear and present our best selves. Easier typed than actually done- I know. It takes practice, but little by little, anyone can become less fearful.

Think about someone you really look up to- a mentor, someone who inspires you or other people. I'm willing to bet they faced the fear of embarrassment and have been judged countless times, but they still aren't afraid to let their personality shine. That's why we like movie stars, rock stars, sports stars, and fictional characters...stars. They didn't let anyone stop them from going after their dreams; we *all* wish we could do the same. That's what inspires people- others who are not afraid to be themselves.

We'll all so afraid of being ourselves! Read that again and look at how ridiculous it sounds...afraid of *ourselves*. What?! Ourselves is all we got, so why, oh why, do we hide who we are in hopes it will protect us from someone judging us? What a waste of so much energy. It's exhausting hiding, isn't it? You may have gotten really good at it, but at the end of the day you'd feel better about yourself if you were freely *yourself*.

Also, and get this, *everyone* is afraid of failing and being made fun of. It's that early human survival instinct again. As early humans, failure would mean death. If you failed to hunt down the wooly mammoth, you would starve to death. Didn't find shelter, freeze to death. Didn't make a good cave painting, kicked out of Cave Art Academy[10]....but those consequences don't exist anymore. But we still have that instinct.

Everywhere we look, people try to fit in and not call attention to themselves. Everyone dresses similarly, talks similarly, and has similar ways of being as their culture and society tells them to be. We're all lemmings following trends trying not to stick out. We all hide our insecurities because we think it makes us weird...I said *we all* because *we all* have insecurities. So sorry, you aren't unique for being insecure.

The uniqueness comes from ignoring them and being your true self, whatever that means to you. When we see someone wearing a crazy outfit, our first response is to judge. But really, judging only comes from our own insecurities of wishing we could be as brave as that person.

Are you feeling inspired yet? OK, great. So you decided you will go for it, be yourself, and you fail, and people laugh, and you mentally know it's not a big deal, but it still stings. Thanks Keith. People laughed at me...now what! [11]

Well, here's the way to never embarrass yourself again. Instead of running for cover and trying to hide your red blushing face and pretending that it never happened, own it. Point out what embarrassing thing you did. Show everyone you recognize it as silly, and move on. No one can make fun of something you already pointed out. This is an outdated example, but it illustrates the point I'm trying to make...

Remember the movie "8 Mile" starring the legendary cinematic actor of the silver screen, Eminem? Well, if you do or don't- at the end of the film, he has to do one more big final contest where he battle raps the movie's

---

[10] I wonder if there were Art Schools for cave drawings

[11] You just felt a human emotion and you are welcome and still alive. So not that bad, huh?

antagonist (meaning he has to make fun of the other person using improvised hip hop lyrics).

In the entire movie, Eminem's character had failure after failure, nothing worked out for poor Slim Shady. So when it came time for that final battle, instead of making fun of the other person, he made fun of himself first:

> *"...I know everything he's 'bout to say against me.*
> *...I do live in a trailer with my mom.*
> *I did get jumped by all six of you chumps."*
> [lots of curse words]
> *Here, tell these people something they don't know about me."*

When the challenger is supposed to respond on his turn, he freezes, and has nothing he can say back, and Eminem walks off into the sunset, end of movie, and awards rain down on the sky.[12]

The purpose of this wasn't to show off Marshall Mathers' rap skills (which usually have some incredible wordplay and multi-syllabic rhymes), but it's a show that if we point out the embarrassing things about ourselves first, no one can say anything.

Just be self-aware of them with a smile, make a joke, and move on. Don't take things too seriously. It's the celebrities who are trying to be "perfect" and take everything too earnestly that the paparazzi make their money off of – such as the always-perfect person who tripped and a curb and everyone laughed at them. But they never highlight comedians because they aren't the ones trying to be perfect and are open to being silly in their lives. Take that cue and do the same for yourself, no matter your industry.

Now I'm not saying don't be serious about what you do. Even as a comedian, I take my art very seriously, but I find the fun in life's situations- make

---

[12] Joking about awards raining, but the movie did actually win an Oscar for best song.

jokes, play, and find the humor in things. You can protect yourself from outside embarrassment if you make a joke first because no one else can do so afterwards without themselves looking like the dumb ones, "Um, yeah, they already said that."

Imagine going through life without embarrassment. Most people are so stuck in their own heads that they won't even notice or care when you step outside your comfort zone, and if they laugh or judge, just laugh it off too. At least you're not afraid to be yourself instead of being stuck in a shell judging everyone. We're less vulnerable than we think we are, so be brave, be yourself, and be free.

So there we have it. A lack of imagination- doesn't exist. Fear of being laughed, who cares! Let's stop living our lives the way other people think we should, and live them the way we feel we want to deep inside. At the very least, it will be a lot more fun than we're having now.

EXERCISE: Verbal Diatribe

Here's another great exercise to allow your brain to stop judging and to prove that you have a billion ideas already at your disposal in your head. It's called Verbal Diatribe.

This shows us that we have plenty of details in our heads if we get out of our own way and just start talking instead of thinking about what to say.

VERBAL DIATRIBE

SKILLS USED: Expanding Upon Subjects + Accessing Unique Memories

HOW TO DO IT
Prepare your phone's stopwatch (or use anything that counts seconds) and a way to quickly get random words (such as a book, random word generator, etc).

CHOOSE A RANDOM WORD
...and immediately start telling a real personal story or memory based off that word. It doesn't have to be funny, organized, or even interesting - just start talking.

KEEP TELLING DETAILS
...about that memory, and once the clock hits 30 seconds, point to another word, and immediately start a new, unrelated story .

REPEAT THE PROCESS
...using new words. Try at least five. Next time you play talk for 45 seconds and then a minute, doing the entire exercise for longer each time.

GOAL: Never run out of things to say, no matter what the subject is.

Tips:

- The stories shouldn't connect. This is all about generating ideas and showing that one person has enough to pull from by their own experiences.

- Your stories don't have to be directly on the subject either, but whatever comes to mind. For example, if the word is *Fishing*, you could say, *"Fishing, makes me think of fish, which reminds me a sushi, and I love sushi..."* It's all about connecting ideas in your mind.

- Try to use emotions and personal opinions on each subject instead of telling us what it is (saying "I love sushi" is better than "Sushi is a food"...we know that but tell us what you think about the subject)

- Go deeper with each subject instead of listing things (a child might tell a story by saying, *"we went to Disney, and had ice cream, and saw Mickey, and went on rides..."* while an adult would say *"so first we get to the park and there is a huge line for parking, where you have to spend $25 just to park!"* Use details that exist in stories to give you juicier things to say)

EXERCISE: Embarrass Yourself

Skills Used:

* Getting out of your comfort zone
* Creating Confidence

One of the assignments for our Level 1 class is to do something on purpose that is embarrassing and outside your comfort zone, and that's what this exercise is. Don't skip it, but actually do it, and you'll see the benefits.

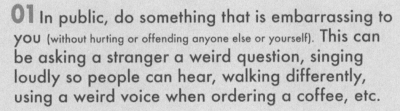

IMPROV EXERCISE

EMBARRASS YOURSELF

How to Do It:

01 In public, do something that is embarrassing to you (without hurting or offending anyone else or yourself). This can be asking a stranger a weird question, singing loudly so people can hear, walking differently, using a weird voice when ordering a coffee, etc.

02 Really, it has to be outside of your comfort zone... and on purpose! Accidentally spilling something doesn't count. Commit and go all the way!

The scariest part of this will be the moment leading up to the embarrassing thing, but once you do it, you'll notice that it wasn't all that bad and that most people around you didn't even care or look at you. The **goal** here is to show you that when you do something embarrassing, it won't be as bad as *thinking* about how embarrassing it might be. In the end, it will give you a sense of empowerment and the confidence to deal with other embarrassing things - which will happen on accident at some point in your life, so you may as well practice it now.

Let go of your expected outcome. Let go of control and need to make it go a certain way. Be brave enough to trust you will be able to ride the waves of whatever way things go. Remember, most people are so stuck in their own heads, they won't even notice or care when you step outside your comfort zone. So, then what's stopping you?

CHAPTER 2

WARM-UPS

Just as professional athletes warm-up before playing a sport or musicians and actors warm-up before a performance, so do improvisers. Each improv warm-up has its own specific function and is helpful to get everyone in an improv group focused, energized, connected, and to relieve anxiety before a performance. Yet, the same exercises can be used before any real-life improvised performance – like a meeting, social event, and basically everything since we don't have any script either. Plus, if you're doing the exercises in this book as you go along, we already did some warm-ups - the previously listed *Shake & Stretch* and *Word Association* are also warm-ups themselves!

Now, if you've never (or actually have) done an improv warm-up before, a lot of them may resemble childish summer camp games, so you may question what you got yourself into. But that's the point; to get you loosened up and be a bit silly so you are able to bring the most to what the performance may require of you. Once we are in an improv scenario, we have to be ready to go! Usually, we show up without any mental or physical preparation and get caught up in the winds of the moment, and that's when things go wrong.

But wait... I thought improv was about non-planning and just being in the moment?

Yes, that's true – partially. We have to exercise our minds to be able to even be free in that present moment. As humans, we used to be naturally present, but with the increasing stress of life, work, and social events, we are usually in our heads more than often. So, these exercises will assist in bringing us back to our natural state. Just as a football player practices running drills, but has to react in the moment during the actual game, practicing these improv drills when we aren't in the 'game of life' will better prepare us for when we are. So knowing all of that, let's go, get loose, and warm-up!

I want to reiterate - the following explanations of some of these warm-ups are really going to seem like I'm describing games that we'd play with children, and all an elaborate prank to see if you'll actually do them and then I'll jump out from behind the couch with a camera and say GOTCHA! But they are real and it's important to take part in the warm-ups no matter how silly they are, because when you do, the silly warm-ups could be fun.

Improv warm-ups fall under four categories of focus and purpose: Energy, Mind, Presence, and Communication. Just like everything else in improv, these were all made up by a bunch of fun, creative people, so feel free to make up your own, but here are some common ones that you can use in the meantime. I've also included some group warm-ups if you are looking for team-building improv exercises to play as well. Most are done in a circle, which doesn't look like we're all in a weird cult to people passing by, but so everyone can easily be visible to each other in the group. Deal with it.

Below is an example of one warm-up per section. I've listed and detailed even more in the back of the book for you as well. Ok, now, for real...let's warm-up!

ENERGY & MOVEMENT WARM-UPS

The goal of warm-ups in this category is to get you out of your head, get your body physically energized, and get blood flowing. You never know what you're going to have to do when the time comes, so it's good to be fully awake in your body and mind. Even if you may not end up performing ballet across the stage (which you could, who knows), chances are you'll at least will have to get up from a chair and walk.

Also, we want to get away from doing "neck-up improv" - meaning that everything you create is forcibly pushed out of your mind after much struggle and thinking hard about what to say or do. Sure, creativity directly comes from synapses firing in our brain, but indirectly, it first comes from elsewhere. So we want it to be inspired by our entire bodies, not just our brains. As human creatures, we have the ability to swing our arms wildly without ever thinking about first doing the action. Isn't that interesting? We're able to do something creative and different without ever planning it, and that's how we want our creative mind to work – to *do* instead of *thinking about doing*. So let's stop thinking so much and play.

EXERCISE: Crazy Eights

This is a simple, and popular and effective improv warm-up to really get the energy flowing.

CRAZY EIGHTS

Skills Used:
* Physicality
* Voice
* Having Fun

How to Do It:

1 With your right hand in the air, shake it furiously eight times counting each number out loud with each shake. *"One, two, three, four, five, six, seven, eight!"*

2 Do the same with the left hand, then right leg, and finally left leg, counting out loud with each.

3 Repeat this process, but this time only counting to seven.

4 Continue until you reach the number one and you instantly feel energized and hyped up.

Goal:

As the numbers decrease, energy should increase. You might count louder, in a different voice, or even shake faster. It's called Crazy Eights for a reason, so get crazy with it and commit!

Tip: Something else you can also focus on with each shake is the anxiety that is being held in your body. Imagine shaking it out so that by the end there is none left. We all hold nervousness in different places in our bodies, so get rid of that stuff.

EXERCISE: Calisthenics

Even simple gm exercises can help warm you up for creativity and communication. And improv!

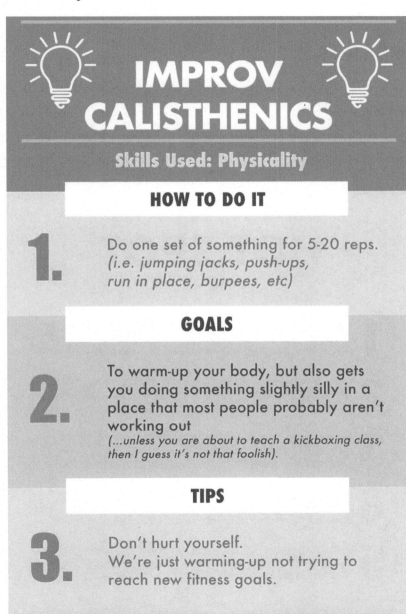

IMPROV CALISTHENICS

Skills Used: Physicality

HOW TO DO IT

1. Do one set of something for 5-20 reps. (i.e. jumping jacks, push-ups, run in place, burpees, etc)

GOALS

2. To warm-up your body, but also gets you doing something slightly silly in a place that most people probably aren't working out (...unless you are about to teach a kickboxing class, then I guess it's not that foolish).

TIPS

3. Don't hurt yourself. We're just warming-up not trying to reach new fitness goals.

MIND WARM-UPS

Just as it's important to have your body warmed up, you also want to have your mind awake and sharp, and that's what the focus is for these mind-bending warm-ups.

EXERCISE: Hot Spot

This is an exercise that people either adore...or never want to do ever again. I invite you to try (at least one time) and really commit to doing it. It's great for getting out of your own way and letting your mind connect to different ideas – plus, it's pretty fun when you let go of self-judgment!

IMPROV EXERCISE
HOT SPOT

Skills Used:
Connecting Ideas, Voice, Having Fun

1 Set a timer for two-minutes

2 Start to sing a song that exists (not a made up one) to the very best of your ability (you don't have to sing *well*)

3 Think of another song that song reminds you of (a related genre, artist or band, a word that was in a lyric...anything)

4 Now start singing that new song, again really commit to the singing - don't phone it in.

5 Keep going until the timer is up or beyond. Next time go for even longer with less pausing in between songs.

Hot Spot Example:

> SONG 1: *"Shot through the heart and you're to blame. You give love a bad name!"*
> SONG 2: *"All you need is love... All you need is love... love is all you need..."*
> SONG 3: *"Let it be, let it be... Let it be, let it be... Whisper words of wisdom, let it be..."*
> SONG 4: *"Let's....let's stay together...lovin' you whether, whether.... times are good or bad, happy or sad...."*

...and the beat goes on....as in the game contuse, not the song, but I guess the song also would work!

The **goals** of this warm-up are to get your mind connecting songs to other songs (just like ideas connect to other ideas in scenes), warm-up your voice, body, and of course, support your own ideas.

As awkward as it is to sing out loud, it's also awkward when you let yourself - and the game – die. Most of us don't know the words to many songs unless they are playing while we are singing them, so we want to switch to new songs as often as we can before we start to lose our energy, forget the rest of the song, and die a slow, painful embarrassing improv death.

PRESENCE WARM-UPS

While the previous section focused on warming up and activating the mind, this section is all about getting present and focused. As we know, the number one rule of improv is to listen, and if you are really being in the moment, you will be able to listen and respond much more efficiently, effectively, and effervescently (oops, not that last one).

These warm-ups focus on that as well as strengthen group chemistry. In improv, it's important to trust and know your fellow performer, so when you're both on stage, you can trust that the other person will support you. Well, the same goes for someone you may be working on a project with or any other group dynamic.

It's like hanging out with your best friend – you know how they speak and the shorthand language they use, and you probably have easy-flowing conversations with them. That's the idea with group chemistry. The more you know someone, have a history with them, and even connect to them in the present moment, the more you will be able to respond quickly to anything that happens.

You probably feel most at ease and the freest to be yourself when you're around people you know. So if you have this sort of relationship with members of your team, you're going to create and think at your best because you feel comfortable, know them very well, and know there will be support for anything.

But even if you don't have a chance to get to know the other person, such as a social event where you are meeting someone for the first time, these warm-ups still strengthen your own presence on being in the moment.

EXERCISE: Breathe with The Second Circle

Skills Used:

* Anxiety-Relief
* Focus

I could write an entirely separate book about the idea of The Second Circle, but I don't have to because somebody else already did. The concept of The Second Circle was created by a theater director from England named Patsy Rodenburg.[13]

For years, she would watch live productions with producers and critics, and they would say about how some Persons on stage just have "It" and "have stage presence" while some other people did not.

So Patsy wanted to discover whether stage presence was something you could gain or whether people were either born with it or not. In her book, she states that there are three possible Circles of Energy that people are in at any given moment.

Being in the space of what she calls First Circle means you're very closed off, and when you're in your own world. You're not aware of stuff going around you and you're really up in your head. If you've ever zoned out doing an activity, such as reading or scrolling on your phone, and didn't notice how much time had passed, you were in First Circle.

On the opposite end of this energy spectrum is the Third Circle, which is more aggressive, but overcompensating, outward energy that almost takes up other people's space. You can think of this as a loud, hostile person you might find at a sports bar... you feel uncomfortable around them, and

---

[13] Patsy Rodenburg, *The Second Circle: How to Use Positive Energy for Success in Every Situation* (W. W. Norton Company, 2008)

they feel like they take your energy, or at worst, might be confrontational, so you stay away.

While both of these Circles have their places and uses in everyday life (read her book to find out more), the place we most want to be for presence is in Second Circle. This Circle meets in the middle of First and Third and is when we are present, in the moment, aware of our surroundings, listening and tuned in to everything around us. If you ever had that feeling after a good mediation or workout, or when you are around someone who you are first in love with, then congrats, you were in Second Circle.

Patsy comes to the conclusion that while some people have a natural presence, you can also strengthen your own with a few exercises. Second Circle exercises such as these that you will read if you keep reading here and don't put the book down and stop reading can also be used as improv warm-ups by yourself or with your group. For each of these exercises, there isn't a tangible goal, such as our other warm ups, but more of a feeling or sensation that you get which will make you present and calm, which means you have successfully entered the Second Circle, and that itself is the goal.

The following Second Circle exercises are not listed in any particular order, usefulness, or effectiveness, but are just numbered for formatting's sake.

SECOND CIRCLE EXERCISE 1

SECOND CIRCLE
EXERCISE 1
How to Do It:

1 Simply walk around the space that you're in
(living room, parking lot, lobby before a big meeting, etc.)

2 As you walk, imagine that every movement you make ripples
outward and touches everything in the space

3 Stay focused on that sensation and try expand what you are
"touching" around you - without actually touching anything

As we walk around, we tend to think that the only thing we're actually touching is our feet to the ground. But really, we are constantly moving through air that has within that "emptiness" millions of molecules and other tiny science stuff we can't see with the naked human eye (put some clothes on your eyes, geez).

So to connect this idea from what we can't see to a sensation that we can feel, as you're walking around, imagine that you were walking through a big room filled with gelatin or water and that every movement you make, big or small, moves the air, molecules, water, or gelatin around you which then moves those things outward, reaching everything else that you aren't physically touching.

You can compare this same idea to jumping into a swimming pool. The water is calm and flat until you yell "Cannonball" and jump in, causing water to splash over other people who were just sunbathing and you get dragged out by the lifeguard because you weren't supposed to be swimming at this time. The point is, that you landed in the middle of the pool, but your motion pushed the water outward to create waves big enough to splash. That's the same idea with this exercise, but it's invisible air molecules instead of visible waves and sour looks from sunbathers.

Another thing we take for granted that we can focus on for this exercise is gravity. We use the gravitational force on Earth literally every moment of our lives, but we aren't consciously aware of it. So as you're walking around in this exercise, try to get the sensation that with each step you take, the floor is holding you up, and you're not floating away into the sky. All because of gravity. Being aware of the air around us or the pull of gravity will make you more present and move you into that Second Circle!

SECOND CIRCLE EXERCISE 2 (again there's no order)

This Second Circle exercise you can do standing completely still or even sitting in a chair (yay laziness!).

For this, it helps to not look at an object that you have an emotional attachment or memory of at first. By looking there might make it harder to focus as your mind will start to think of that emotion or memory instead of focusing on the sensation of breathing with the object itself.

Once you get used to doing this with a more random object, then by all means, please do it with an object that you have emotions with because it will only heighten those emotions. Even try breathing with and to someone you love; the connection will be incredible...but only if they feel the same way back. Doing this to that barista you have a crush on is going to be super creepy, so please don't.

SECOND CIRCLE

EXERCISE 2

HOW TO DO IT

1. Focus on an object out of your reach, but not so far away that you can't really see it. This could be a tree, or a hanging picture, or weird mark on the wall, etc.

IMAGINE

2. ...yourself sending your breath to that object. Even if it's an inanimate object, you can still imagine it breathing with you - and if that seems weird, get over it because we're doing improv which is all about imagination!*

BREATHE DEEP

3. ...until you feel connected or as if you were physically touching that object, even though you haven't moved at all. Once you get this sensation you will feel very present, and thus in Second Circle.

*Even if you we can't see our breath, it's very real - so imagine the tiny particles of air being sent to the object if that helps you.

SECOND CIRCLE EXERCISE 3 (randomly placed third!)

EXERCISE 3
SECOND CIRCLE

1 Stand straight up, then completely bend over at your hips, and let your body loosely hang.

2 Grab each of your shoulders with the opposite hand and let your elbows hang freely.

3 Focus on a spot on the floor and breath deeply to that spot, breathing from your abdomen instead of cheat.

4 After 8 breaths to that spot, let your arms hang completely down as loose as possible.

5 Slowly stand up, stacking one vertebra of your spine on top of the other as you do and deeply breathing until standing.

6 Once fully up, slowly look around. If you did this correctly, you will feel very present and in Second Circle.

When you reach the moment of being in the Second Circle with these exercises, the moment may be fleeting. That's expected. We normally aren't in this circle of energy, so our mind quickly brings us back to where we usually are- thinking of other stuff or even having the thought, "Hey, look at that, I'm in Second Circle, this worked." – which means you actually went back to First Circle and aren't being present in Second. Funny how the mind works.

While these are excellent warm-ups you can do before some unknown situation, they are also good to do any time you feel stressed, whether before a job interview or going into a social engagement or a meeting. Relax yourself into the Second Circle is a great way to bring your best self forward.

Some people have compared this concept to meditation, and while it has some parallels, the Second Circle by Patsy Rodenburg is its own powerful technique.

Want t know more? Then go check out the book "The Second Circle" by Patsy Rodenburg. It may just change your life.

COMMUNICATION WARM-UPS

For these games, we will be making up conversations with another person while also working on different rules for each game.

Before we go on, I want to point out that these made-up conversations you are having in this game are exactly like playing an improv scene (both people aren't sure what to say and are interacting and making it up as they go along). So in these games, you don't have to be yourself, sitting in a chair, in this office, doing an exercise with a co-worker- but can *pretend* to be anyone and anywhere! It's way more fun to pretend to be two explorers sailing a ship through a storm instead of two people in a cold office. Try expanding your imagination and imagine you're having a conversation in these made-up circumstances. What types of things might those explorers say in that situation? This will be way more fun too.

EXERCISE: Where Have My Fingers Been

Skills Used:

* Continuing Conversations
* Having Fun

This is an exercise that works on improvising a conversation that your fingers will be having with each other, and since you are only using your fingers, don't put any pressure on yourself for it to be that funny, or even that interesting for that matter, but only to have a short pretend conversation between two people (here being your fingers).

IMPROV EXERCISE

WHERE HAVE MY FINGERS BEEN

How to Do It:

01 Get a random location (use a random location generator website so you can't cheat)

02 Do a quick back-and-forth conversation pretending two of your fingers are talking to each other in that location.

03 Each finger say a minimum of three lines, a total of six. But feel free to say more!

04 Using another random location, start a new conversation, and repeat the process.

Fingers Example: Location: Aquarium

> LEFT-HAND FINGER: *I wonder how cold the water is in the shark tank.*
>
> RIGHT-HAND FINGER: *Probably pretty war since it says these sharks are from the Gulf of Mexico.*
>
> LEFT-HAND FINGER: *I'm going to dip my toe in to find out.*
>
> RIGHT-HAND POINTER FINGER: *Um, there are multiple reasons why you shouldn't do that, but I'd love to see what happens.*

The **goal** here is to relieve the pressure of having to have a good back-and-forth conversation and just to start creating a simple one. Many first-time improvisers will think an improv scene is so difficult and confusing to even try to attempt, so getting that first one out of the way is a huge relief. This counts!

Again, just think what people might do or say while in that setting. It doesn't have to be that long or life-changing of a conversation, but just a made up conversation that could happen.

Tips:

- Don't try to think of a 'good location' to give yourself an easier time. The more random the setting, the better to get the most out of the game.

Advanced Version:

- Bonus points if you give your finger-characters different voices and emotions!
- Practice this game in a public setting like a bank or grocery store, and you'll be sure to get stared at or thrown out. Please don't get arrested, and if you do, I claim no responsibility.

So there's a bunch of exercises and warm-ups you can get started on (and I listed even more in the back of this book). Keep practicing them and keep some in your back pocket to use before stepping into those unknown circumstances – they will keep you focused, less stress-filled, and ready to respond to anything unknown that comes your way.

CHAPTER 3
THE RULES OF IMPROV

"**S**o do anything and say anything, and there's no wrong answer. Got it! Now I'm an improv expert!" Not just yet.

Before we run out into the world with our new sense of creative freedom, we have to walk through a few rules. Improv is possible because it follows guidelines that assist situations to move forward. Without them, there would be far less chances of scenarios working and higher chances that they would devolve into arguments and confusion and who wants to try to converse and deal with that? So, while no one knows what is going to happen before an improvised, unknown moment (if they did, then it's not improv, right), following these rules will help us become much more successful in navigating uncharted waters.[14]

If you were to look up "Improv Rules" online or in other books, there would be varying lists, sometimes ten, sometimes five, sometimes twenty, with different orders, and some saying theirs are the best and the only true rules. All of those are fine, but I like to use these simple four:

Rule #1: Listening

Sure we know how to hear, but how well do we listen, as in *active listening*? Everything we need when improvising is in reaction to what someone just said. The more and more I teach, perform, and watch improv, the more it

---

[14] I cannot confirm that these rules actually will work in navigating the ocean, but I have a feeling they won't.

becomes abundantly clear; improv is in it's simplest terms: Someone says something, then someone responds.

That's it. That's all there is to it. Put the book down and go on with your life (but don't we have much more to cover).

We don't know what the other person is going to say until they say it, and we shouldn't know what we're going to say yet, either. Everything created in an improv situation should be from moment-to-moment, and if we aren't fully listening to the other person, we'll miss things.

Think about all the times we've met someone and immediately forgot their name. Someone literally spoke their name seconds ago, but we already forgot it? No, we didn't forget it because we never heard it in the first place. We're too busy thinking of the past or what to say in the future and miss everything right in the present. This proves that to truly listen, it has to be active and not just letting our ears do all the work for us.

So much information can be taken from how someone says something as much as what they actually say. If someone says "good morning" in sadness, it's different from saying "good morning" in anger. And all that subtext and information can inform the situation and our response just by simply listening and allowing ourselves to react.

Another example: you're driving down the road, and the car behind you lets out an extended honk and speeds around you. I'm willing to bet you reacted in some way – probably anger, or maybe confusion, or even laughter – but you reacted. Your body and mind already react before you even think about it. That honk brought you into the present time, and you couldn't help not hearing it and reacting. Treat all your scenes this way too (listening in the moment, not having road rage).

We cannot do any of the other improv rules without fully listening. But now that we covered that onto...

Rule #2: Agreement

You may have heard of this one before in what is called "Yes, And" as it's the most common rule in all of the improv universe. It's commonly listed as the first rule, but how can we agree to something if we aren't listening in the first place? So it's my second rule instead.

Agreement and *Yes, And* simple means to agree to the ideas and circumstances you and the other person have created. Once something is said, it IS truth, and then we add more information, opinions, thoughts, and details to build off of that to continue. Since when people are performing improv, no one knows what's going to happen, by agreeing and adding more information, the made-up scenario can move forward instead of just being a confusing ball of what is going on. For example, here is an improvised scene *without* using an agreement

> PERSON 1: *Here is the pizza you ordered!*
> PERSON 2: *That's not a pizza, that's a tire.*
> PERSON 1: *I know, just kidding, it's a tire for your car.*
> PERSON 2: *But I don't have a car.*
> PERSON 1: *...I know, I meant it's for a tire swing.*
> PERSON 2: *But you're not holding anything. Your hands are empty.*
> PERSON 1: *...Right, it's invisible.*
> PERSON 2: *No it's not.*

Do you see where this scene is going? Nowhere at all. The hardest thing to do in improv is to come up with that first idea, which Person 1 did nicely by offering the pizza. But Person 2 denied that reality, and the scene died, and Person 1 had to do all the heavy lifting of coming up and justifying things. Chances are they'll never want to do a scene with that other person again, and a future friendship will be lost! But when we agree to the made-up situations and build from that truth, we get one like example full of agreement:

> PERSON 1: *Here is the pizza you ordered!*
> PERSON 2: *About time! You're late, and that means the pizza is free!*
> PERSON 1: *That is our policy, sir, but please don't tell my boss.*
> PERSON 2: *Oh, what's in it for me?*
> PERSON 1: *I'll throw in these free breadsticks.*
> PERSON 2: *Deal. I'm glad you carry around extra breadsticks with you for situations just like this.*

Now, this scene is going somewhere! All because Person 2 agreed to the made-up situation and added their own information (you're late, so the pizza is free). Then we have a nice pattern going of Person 2 blackmailing the delivery person into giving them more free stuff, including my very silly last line above.

We can further the scene by agreeing and adding to the made-up situation. Once something is said, it's true. Even if we had something else in our mind first – if the other person establishes something else, drop that idea and work with what was said only.

So, how does this work in real-life? The same idea applies. Instead of trying to devise a solution for a problem or idea by ourselves, we can build it together. For example, you and a friend are deciding what food to eat:

> PERSON 1: *I'm hungry. How about we get Thai food.*
> PERSON 2: *No, I don't want Thai.*
> PERSON 1: *OK, how about Mexican?*
> PERSON 2: *No, not that.*

> PERSON 1: *Ramen?*
> PERSON 2: *Nah.*

In this example, Person 1 had to do all the creation of ideas while Person 2 didn't help at all, and the two are either never going to eat, or get mad at eat other – both things are not fun. But with *Yes, And* things will work much better...

> PERSON 1: *I'm hungry. How about we get Thai food.*
> PERSON 2: *I had Thai food yesterday, but I know a good place with a bunch of options. Let's try that.*
> PERSON 1: *Yes, I love options!*

Now they're eating!

..."But wait, those people didn't agree in that situation! Now I'm really confused." Oh, good noticing, random reader. Here's a little thing I've learned along the way that was never taught to me, which I call "Advanced Yes, And." We don't have to agree to every detail but agree that it was said and build off of it.

"Huh?"

People in an improv situation don't have to actually say the words "Yes, And" to everything that's happening. They can, but they can also be in disagreement, as long as the people agree with the common goal and move forward.

So, with the above example, they were agreeing they were hungry and that they were going to get food, and instead of completely blocking by saying, "No, I had Thai food yesterday" and leaving it up to the other person to find the solution, they basically said "*Yes*, I just had that food, *and* I know a place that offers other things – so still *Yes, And*ing!

Yes, And butts up right against the common phrase *Yes, But* where someone says they agree, then says *But...* which really means them saying *no*. This is our go-to reaction to things because we don't want to let go of control. We want to pilot the plane, not let go, and build it in collaboration with others. But that's not how the beauty and freedom of improv work. Improv works when a group of people agrees on a common goal. So let go of control, agree, and see where things can take us that we would have never ended up on our own.

Even if you don't fully agree to something, like trying to create an idea or solve a problem, if everyone Yes, Ands and builds forward together and you still reach a dead end, you can always start over. But chances are you will reach something new that would have never been created by one mind alone. The power of *Yes, And* is that it combines the thoughts and ideas of multiple people and usually creates something totally fresh and unknown.

This is a great technique to use in conversation as well. Instead of trying to think of our own stuff to say, just Yes, And off of what was said by the other person (by first, of course, listening). For example:

> PERSON 1: *Work's been a bit slow lately*
> PERSON 2: *Yeah, I always wonder why it ebbs and flows like that.*
> PERSON 1: *Right? It's like just been even instead of some days busy and some not.*
> PERSON 2: *You ever have days so busy that time flies by?*
> PERSON 1: *Absolutely!*

Aw, that's sweet – look at them conversing so well using Yes, And.

Well, I know what you're thinking now...what about when the other person doesn't agree and says no to everything?

When we find one of these control-freaks, it's time to Yes, And even more. They are holding onto the controls so tightly because they feel like their ideas are never heard, and their ego is so stubborn that they won't listen to anyone's ideas but their own. But...what if they think something you say was one of their ideas. For example, someone is getting notes on a design project:

> DESIGNER: *Here's the logo with green on the outside.*
> STUBBORN PERSON: *No, it should be black.*
> (...a denial.)
> DESIGNER: *Oh, I like that, to make the other colors inside stand out more.*
> (a good Yes, And move.)
> STUBBORN PERSON: *I don't like green.*
> (...another denial.)
> DESIGNER: Perfect. *So we can add a darker color in there.*
> (...yet another good Yes, And move.)
> STUBBORN PERSON: *Great idea!*
> (me).

...and now they agreed to darker, which could be dark green, and they thought it was their idea, and both parties are happy. See? Yes, And allows us to navigate and build off of what comes our way, instead of butting heads of both sides wanting it specifically their way and noting else.

Ok, enough on agreement? Agreed.

Rule #3: Support & Trust

The third improv rule is Support. Support yourself and the other person. Since the hardest thing is to create that very first moment (as we've said), we want to support and trust that whatever you or the other person says is the best idea to follow in that moment, and work together to grow a great scenario.

Don't judge what pops into your head. When we practice improv, we're really training our instincts for creating spontaneous ideas- so if your instincts are telling you to do something, trust them! Whatever comes into your head is correct (there is no wrong answer, but no answer)[15]. Stop judging and thinking there must be a better idea to go with...we'll keep saying it until you get it!

The more you practice the skills of improv, the more you'll find that every situation and opportunity to improvise is a temporary moment. No matter how terrible or how wonderful an improv situation goes, it only existed in that specific moment. Sure, you can record it or tell someone about it, but it's a pure form of itself. Improv only exists right here and now.

So with that, know that you'll have other opportunities to make situations better, wittier, more creative, or whatever – there will always be another chance to improvise again. So stop stressing trying to make this one right now so dang perfect! It can never be perfect because *we're making it up*. It can be better than others, but perfection doesn't exist in improv. Go back in time and ask Miles Davis if his improvised jazz with John Coltrane was ever perfect. Nope! It may have created some of the greatest jazz recordings ever, but perfect he would agree it is not.

To walk one step even further, no circumstances can ever be perfect! Perfect is subjective; while some people think one thing is amazing, others could care less about it. So stop trying to think and overthink and be perfect. Enjoy the moment of spontaneous interaction, make it the best

---

[15] But don't use this as a soapbox to spit a bunch of offensive stuff. No no.

you can, look at how to you can get better *next time*, and then let me use your time machine.

So support your ideas as they arise and the other person's ideas.

Let's say someone starts a conversation about driving in a car.[16] Instead of thinking, "Ugh, I don't want to talk about driving and I have a better idea that I'm going to push instead!" embrace their ideas completely and go along for the ride (pun intended!).

Trust and support everything that happens, whether you came up with it or not. If you leave the person you are interacting with out to die because you don't like or have much knowledge of their subject, you will never get better at using improv skills. Again, if it turns out terrible, you will know how to do better next time. Failing is part of the process as we teach our brains to think differently. Instead, embrace the unknown and use it as a chance to work on these skills. This all really goes back to Yes, And. Let go of your control and see where this moment takes you.

Lastly, Trust also means trusting the process of learning. Improv is a skill that anyone can learn, but like any skill, it takes some time, takes some failures along the way, and will have good days and bad days (or conversations and interactions). But trust that as long as we keep trying and learning from our missteps, we will get better. So keep going...onto the next rule.

Rule #4: Assume

This rule can also be said as "Don't Ask Questions" or don't say "I Don't Know" or to "Assume Information." When two people are improvising in a moment, nobody knows what's going to happen next...that's why it's

---

[16] Which every improviser will do at least 100 times during their improv careers.

improv. Even if someone starts the conversation with lots of energy and saying a lot of information, that still doesn't mean they know every moment of what's going to happen next.

So, since both people are equally non-knowledgeable and in the dark about how the rest of the course of events will go, each person has the same responsibility to fill in the blanks. If something hasn't been clearly established, then there's an opportunity to add information, and while no one knows anything because it's made up, assume that you do know.

For example, if in an improv scene, it hasn't been established where the situation is taking place, and because the other person doesn't know any more than you do about the scene, instead of asking a question like "Where are we again?" Change that question into a statement like "Starbucks is always so busy." So assume you know instead of asking.

Look, in real life, no one would ever ask where they were if they were standing in a Starbucks, but in improv, this happens all the time, usually because one performer is too nervous about making a choice and worried that their idea isn't going to be good. I'll say it again, and probably more times as we go on, there's no wrong answer except for no answer, so you just have to say something. On the flip side, if you make a statement instead of asking a question, your improv scene partner will feel relieved because now both of you know more about the scene and get to the fun of playing in it.

Saying *I don't know* or asking empty questions in a situation, puts all of the work on the other person to come up with stuff to talk about. Get used to making statements and adding information as if you already know. If we make a statement instead of asking questions, the other person is going to feel relieved because now both of you are building something together. On the flip side, answering *I don't know* if you get asked a question really doesn't help any conversation move forward. Making a statement adds more information to it and gives both parties more to talk about.

Wait, you said *empty questions*... what does that mean? Oh no, I asked a question! I ruined improv! Noooooo!

Relax. Some questions can be asked as long as it adds information. For example:

> PERSON 1: *Hello, may I inquire if you serve roasted lamb here at this dining establishment?*
>
> vs.
>
> PERSON 1: *Hello, what is there?*

In the first very fancy example, the person asked a question, yes, but there was lots of information in the question. It doesn't put the other person in the hot seat to name a bunch of foods.[17] And here's the thing, if you had the words "roasted lamb" in your question, it would allow the other person's mind to connect to more ideas and build from there as well – thinking about what that word makes you think of.

Here's another thing I learned along the way – people ask questions because they are nervous about making the wrong choice, but they also ask questions because they don't think they know enough about a subject or person in which they are talking about. And this is where the Assume comes in.

If we fully listen to what the other person is saying, we can also *assume* lots of information about them. Going back to a previous example, if someone says "good morning" in sadness, instead of just replying "Good

---

[17] Many times food comes up in improv, probably because we'd all rather be eating than working on new mind muscles. It happens.

morning" and going about your day, notice how they gave you a huge clue of a path you can go down to talk more, all by assuming. You may ask a follow-up question (that has details) – "You sound a bit down. Everything going okay?" – and now a conversation is moving.

We can assume a lot from what words someone says or how they say those words. If someone tells us excitedly that yesterday they brought their dog to the dog park, we can assume that 1) they have a dog, 2) they usually don't go to the dog park, since if it was routine, why would they choose to mention it 3) something exciting happened there. We can then respond by matching their excitement and asking how it went, instead of thinking of what to say next and changing the subject, as all too many of us commonly do. By being present and aware of the other person, listening and assuming information, it's impossible to run out of things to say!

Yes, I'm now saying questions are acceptable, but because they are going off of what we heard (listening), and that's appropriate. So don't get too in your head about asking questions or not. Just don't use asking questions as a crutch to make the other person do all the work while you don't say anything else. Making statements is always better for both sides.

Now I know you are probably now thinking 'but I was always told not to assume something' or 'assuming makes an ass out of you and me.'

While that last statement is a cute play-on-words, assuming is actually a helpful skill to leverage, as long as you assume with curiosity. I'm not suggesting you assume something and then accept that as a fact and move on- not at all.

But when we assume with curiosity, we make assumptions the best we can, which then sets up the other person to either agree with you ("oh, you're exactly right, I am...") or – sometimes even better – they will correct you.

As much as people are afraid of being wrong, is just as equal to how much people enjoy being right. So, if you make a wrong assumption – with curiosity – the other person will correct you, and now you have more information than you had before – information that you know for a fact is correct because *they told you*!

Using our example of someone saying "Good morning" with a hint of sadness, if you reply with "You sound a bit down, everything going okay?" and are wrong, they will tell you! "Oh yeah, I'm fine, just really tired because my usual coffee place was closed today."

Boom! Now you know they usually go to the same coffee place every morning and can continue the conversation from that- information you wouldn't have had if you didn't assume, and much better than what most people do, which is to talk about themselves or move onto a different subject. Use what's right in front of our faces and Listen and Assume with curiosity!

By assuming with curiosity, I mean saying it is a curious way – like asking a light question with your statement (such as the example of "You seem a bit down..."). You aren't stating this a definitive fact, but making a light assumption to continue the conversation and learn more about the other person.

Because of this, the next time someone tells you it's bad to assume, smile and assume that you'll be better at talking to people because you now know that assumptions are actually powerful tools...when done right...as I just told you too.

So dems da rules. There they are. These, again, are guidelines are to help us along the path of making stuff up. All of these rules are based on ones created in some kitchen by the Compass Players,[18] when their members found that a lot of improv scenes included people not listening and arguing about the reality of what they're making up. So they came up with these to let the creativity move forward and get to more interesting scenarios. Learn these rules front and back until they become second nature, and then, maybe, just maybe, you can learn to break them too.[19]

---

[18] One of the first "improv groups" that included Elaine May, Mike Nichols, Del Close among other fantastic actors.

EXERCISE: Listen to The Moment

A simple and almost meditative exercise to bring us back to the present moment and prepare us to listen, and thus respond from there instead of from our overactive thinking mind.

Listen to This Moment

SKILLS USED: Focus + Listening + Being Present + Relaxation

1 **HOW TO DO IT**
Right now, take this moment and really listen. Hear if you can notice all the sounds in the room. Don't label them, don't judge them, you don't even have to question what they are; just hear them. Really try to hear as many different sounds as you can as if you were listening to a beautiful piece of music.

2 **FOCUS**
...now on the silences between the sounds. Hear how some sounds come and go or maybe there's never complete silence, but still there are moments of somewhat-silence between every sound.

3 **FEEL**
...your body now in this room while your are still listening. Try not to shift or change anything about your body, just feel it being present in the room.

4 **LOOK**
...around the room or at your hands. You might notice things that you haven't really noticed before. Right now you are in the present moment.

GOAL: open up our listening while really being present and not letting our brain get distracted by everything around us.

EXERCISE: Yes, And Story

This great exercise shows us how easy Yes, And is and how powerful it is to create new ideas and can be done with a group or on our own.

YES, AND STORY

Skills Used: Listening + Agreement + Idea Generation

HOW TO DO IT

1. Start with any random statement. It doesn't have to be exciting, in fact it's good if it's even boring.

SAY YES

2. Say the word YES, and repeat that previous statement.

NOW AND

3. Say the word AND then continue the story with the next logical thing that can come next

KEEP GOING

4. Do the same thing again by *Yes, And-ing* that last statement, and continue the story as long as you like. Try to go longer each time.

I want you to say the word Yes before repeating the statement because it puts the sentence right in front of our brains and allows us to react to it specifically. You cannot help but respond to what you just said if you're fully focused on it. Without this vital part of the exercise, it's easy for your mind to start to think of where you want the story to go next and not fully listen to what you just said.

Our **goal** here is to demonstrate that we can use anything as a jumping off point, and as long as we agree and add to everything created, it will bring us to an interesting place that we wouldn't have otherwise reached.

Tips:

- You don't have to remember and repeat every statement that was said before the last one, but only the one that came right before. It's an exercise in building, not memorization.
- It's best to add the next logical thing that can happen in the story after you say And. Sure, aliens can show up and vaporize all of humanity after saying I like the outdoors, but let's stick to the simple, most obvious choices right now instead. It's better to focus on building off of the last thing said than trying to show off how creative you can be. That comes later.
- Lastly, be sure to say *And* instead of *But*. Saying *But* is a slight denial in the statement that was said. It means that- yes, this statement happened, but you wish it hadn't so you can go with your own idea of where you wanted the story to go. You can only build off of what was last said, so trying to guide the story in a preconceived concept is definitely not improvisation. Go with the flow!
- Try starting with the most boring, uneventful sentence you want. This game shows that no matter where you begin, *Yes, Anding* can make anything more interesting.

CHAPTER 4
HOW TO DO A SCENE

Great, so now we know anyone can improvise and and how we just have to use our own experiences... but...what do we do in an actual improv situation? If there is no wrong answer, does that mean I can do anything at all?

Whoa, calm down, relax, and stop asking so many questions. (hey, that's one of our rules!) To navigate the waters when you find yourself in an unexpected improv situation, we first have to explore how to do an improv scene.

Don't stress about this! We already talked about the above, and it's also not about being funny. Even if you never want to play an imaginary circumstance of an improv scene or think it's 'too much about acting' trust me here when I say the way an "improv comedy scene" works on stage in front of an audience is the same way an improv situation plays out, whether it be a conversation or a presentation or (insert your own here). If anything, when we're able to handle doing an improv scene, where we could end up pretending to be a singing table monster – I have really witnessed this – then when we're in a situation where we're playing ourselves (real life) it will be that much simpler. To make this chapter make more sense in our brain, we could replace the word "scene" with "situation" or "scenario" and all the same rules would apply. But stick, and I promise by the end I will connect all of this to real-world situations either way. Deal? Great.

Doing an improv scene is actually pretty easy if you know what to do. There's a difference between good and bad improv scenes, just as there are good and bad conversations, presentations, and anything, really. Even though we are just making it up, we can still learn skills and techniques to turn these "make-em-ups"[20] better.

Earlier we compared improv to playing football. Both have practices where players learn and run drills and play over and over, but at game time, no one knows exactly what's going to actually happen. Players are just using their trained instincts from doing countless drills and using each player's skill set in that moment. We learn the rules, techniques, and what not-to do, but once performing a scene, we just have to let it go and be in the moment. So being here, right now, in this moment, let's talk about scenes more. So here we go...

The First Two Lines

The information about what is happening in your scene is all known within the first two sentences spoken. Yeah, that's it, two little lines, and even sometimes less. This is why... an improv scene is literally:

> PERSON 1: says something (anything)
> PERSON 2: responds.

That's really all it is. Within that time, you should have a good idea of who these people are, how they know each other, and what will most likely happen next in the scene. Here's an example:

> PERSON 1: *Help! My Cat's stuck in the tree!*
> PERSON 2: *I'll help you.*

---

[20] What some improvisers refer to improv as. Ironically, of course

In its most simplified version, this scene is about someone who needs help, and someone who is helpful, so without trying to figure out what to do, we simply follow down this path we have already created. So it'd continue with Person 1 needing more help, and Person 2 helping them. Let's even look at this example - which includes a straight-up breaking-the-rules denial "bad improv" move.

> PERSON 1: *Help! My Cat's stuck in the tree!*
> PERSON 2: *No, it's not, you don't have a cat.*

A terrible denial of the reality there by saying they don't have a cat, but it still works. Simply put, this scene is either about Person 1 being crazy, maybe in an insane asylum, and Person 2 being their caretaker (maybe the next line is "Please, you need to take your medication"), OR it could also be Person 1 needs help, and Person 2 just won't look up in the tree, they are blind, or they are the crazy one. Even though making people crazy in improv is a lazy move, either way, this example can work and move forward, and it's all within the first two lines.

This is why.

Whatever we do at the start of a scene signifies our *character* (or persona) for the remainder of that scene. No one knows what's going to happen in the scene, but once we do *something*, we just have to become aware of *that which we did* and then hold onto it. This is easiest understood by describing *that thing that we did* as an emotion or adjective.

In the first example above, we had someone whose emotion is *helpless* and someone who is *helpful*. That's who these people are, in this moment, so we hold onto that reality (*Yes, And* it, buddy!) and keep doing more of what we already did with those emotions to keep the scene moving forward from there. It's really that simple.

Was that simple for you? If not, let me explain it a bit more and in different words. Whatever feeling you have at the start of the interaction, notice what it was, and do more from that emotion. Most scenes go bad early on because people aren't *listening* to each other (or themselves) and have no idea what they did at the very start. They are constantly looking for what the scene is about and what to do next, even though it passed them by seconds ago. All you have to do is notice what you did, hold onto that, and do more of the same within those emotional parameters.

The faster we identify our emotion, the easier it'll be for us to keep talking and doing the scene. If we notice that we are *happy*, then in every sentence that comes our way, we have to respond with *happiness*.

> PERSON 1: *You won a million dollars*
> PERSON 2 (Happy): *Awesome!*
>
> PERSON 1: *Give me all your money or I'll shoot you!*
> PERSON 2 (Happy): *Awesome!*

Yes, even in that second example, we keep our original emotion! The common mistake is to change our emotion for each line we hear. If we do that, we'll be searching for what the scene is about the entire, well, scene. Stick with our emotion and *do not let go*. Every time our emotion changes, it's as if we are starting the scene over, and we'll never have a solid foundation to stand on. Stick with your emotion and do not let go.

An improv scene is only a small window in a moment of time for these made-up characters. It's not a three-minute character arc where someone learns their lessons and changes. No human in the history of humanity would do that in real life. If someone is bummed, they will be bummed for at least a few hours, so I think we can keep that going for a few minutes in an improv scene. Stick with your emotion and do not let go. Should I say it again? I might...

Improv scenes are about how two people relate to each other and how their different emotions interact - either well or poorly, it doesn't matter. Even if both people were the same emotion, they're off to a great start as long as they hold onto it. Stick with your emotion and do not let go. There, I did it!

Now, what if we don't find our emotion within the first two lines? Are we up a creek? No... as long as we find it soon. We get some wiggle room between four to six sentences to really find our emotion. But after three lines each and no emotion has been established, we're getting into dangerous territory. If we don't know our "thing" in the scene, then we will most likely be very lost very soon. Make a choice, any choice, and stick to it.

Never be middle of the road or ambiguous. Make a decision and follow it. There's nothing worse than being in a scene (or conversation, for that matter) with someone who just "Yesses" everything but adds no "And." The *And* is how your character reacts to the situation laid in front of them. React and do something! Most people won't make a clear choice in their scene because they aren't sure what to do or worry if it's a good enough choice. Hello, THERE'S NO WRONG ANSWER BUT NO ANSWER. And not adding anything is a non-answer. Do something...please. It doesn't matter what. Even if you hate it, your scene will be over in a few minutes, and you'll learn from it.

How To Find Your Emotion

Stick with your emotion and do not let go – we get it... okay...but how do we find that emotion? Easy, and you have choices. There are two ways to get our emotion; either thinking of them beforehand, or letting our body language inspire it. Let's go through them.

The only thing we can think up before an improv scene and for it still to work is our own emotion (if you tried to think of what the scene is about and force that idea after the other person initiates with something else, it's going to be a complete mess). But starting with a pre-conceived emotion will work because any emotion can fit over any idea.

Think of some emotions... really, think of three...now how could we respond through the filter of that emotion to each of these statements?

> PERSON: *I burnt the dinner.*
> PERSON: *Looks like you're going to replace the transmission.*
> PERSON: *I think I love you.*

I have no idea our emotions, but I'm betting each one gave us a way to respond to those statements. Again, even if normally we would reply differently – like maybe *mad* or *disappointed* at the burnt dinner, if your pre-planned emotion was *excited*...stick with that! Changing it is even more pointless if you went through all the mental energy to think up an emotion. Any emotion will work. Sure, you may think some are easier, but you aren't reading a book on how to get better at a skill because you want things to be easy – you want to grow, which is difficult at the start but gets easier the more you do.

We can use this same concept outside of an improv comedy scene. Instead of going into an improv scenario unaware of our emotion, pick one to have and then everything we do and say comes from that place. How much better would that networking conversation go if we played *confident*, instead of *nervous-by-default*? Even if we aren't really feeling that way, act like we are...much like we are practicing in these made up improv scenes... see it's all connecting.

But, we can know our emotion even before we say anything, in less than two lines, which requires no active thinking at all, and that's by using our body language. If you have your arms crossed and are looking down at the other person, you're probably a higher status character who is *upset* at someone. Or, if you have your head down and your arms clasped in front of you, you're probably lower status, maybe begging someone not to do something, or you feel guilty. Emotions can be found before we even say anything! Magic! Not really. But what's really easy here is that our bodies can move without us consciously thinking about moving them.

Do something with your arm right now... see? I just said a command, but you made your arm do something specific – maybe it was to flap it, or hold it out in front of you, or whatever. The thing you did wasn't thought about beforehand, but just happened. We do this all time in our lives, too, giving off unspoken emotions through our body language. We mostly aren't aware of it, but still, respond as such to these silent communicators.

Try it for yourself in these two ways: try walking through a grocery store, chest out, arms flared, and making eye contact with everyone you see. Chances are they will move out of your way and not look back at you. You can also just watch people around you and identify their emotions based solely on their body language. It's everywhere. You can assume how people are just from how they are standing. Test this out in everyday life so you'll get better at when the time comes, and instead of going into that interview with your head down, closed off, because you are nervous – you can still tall and match the people you have seen in real life who look as confident as the way you want to come off.

Emotion, emotion, emotion. Trust that once you have that emotion, you'll never run out of stuff to do or say because it all stems from the emotion itself. Use the exercises at the end of this chapter to strengthen our ability to express different emotions beyond the ones we normally do now.

EXERCISE: Character Walk

This is a classic acting exercise, so if you've ever taken an acting class, chances are that you've done this before. However, our focus here is not necessarily acting, but using posture to create an emotion or status.

CHARACTER WALK

SKILLS USED: Physicality + Emotions

1 **HOW TO DO IT**
Get up and simply walk around your space. Whether it's a studio apartment or a conference hall, it doesn't matter. All you have to do is mill about without thinking about anything...yet. Just start moving.

2 **LEAD WITH A BODY PART**
Now have your walking be led by a specific body part. For example, if you lead with your chest- really exaggerate walking with your chest out. You probably don't usually walk like this, so it should feel unnatural and weird.

3 **CONNECT TO AN EMOTION**
This different feeling in your body can now inspire an emotion or adjective. If you're giving the most focus to your chest, it might make you think of someone who is tough or confident or cocky. Or if you lead with your fingers, you might think of someone who is delicate or upper class. Whatever YOU feel is correct.

4 **RETURN TO NORMAL**
After you walk around for a few minutes with that posture, go back to walking normally again. Notice how different it feels.

5 **DO IT AGAIN**
Now lead with a different part of the body. Do this a few times with different body parts and then start to add dialogue as you walk with that emotion, just talking out loud - imagining what this type of person might say, all filtered through that emotion.

GOAL: Inspire new ways of holding yourself, related to different emotions.

As usual, there is no wrong answer except for no answer unless you are thinking about a specific idea or person. The **goal** here is not to think of an idea or a specific person- such as a 'football player' or the 'Prime Minister'- but to think of adjectives and emotions while changing your physicality. So if you do have people come to mind, think of what descriptive words you can use for them. A 'football player' might be *tough* and that would work.

The reason not to get specific for a person is that if you were to use this concept for walking into an improv scenario with a posture and you were thinking 'football player,' that wouldn't help you much (unless you were trying to sneak into a football locker room).

But, if you took on the posture of *acting tough*, anything that comes your way, you'd be able to respond through the lens of the emotion of toughness and use it in any situation. A tough presenter or tough friend takes the essence of a 'football player' but removes any specifics. So think adjectives and descriptive emotions over specific people.

Advanced Version:

You can do a monologue as the character, saying something that they might be telling someone else, or you can simply just pretend you're walking down the street and passing people. How would this character greet others through this emotion? Again, the idea here is seeing how posture and changing your physicality can inspire and lead to emotions for your scenes.

Tips:

- By leading with a different body part, you can think about giving the most energy to that part, or as if a string is pulling it or if you were to walk into a wall (please don't) this would be the first thing that would come in contact the wall.

- You can use this in times when you are feeling less confident as well. Notice how you might walk closed off with your head down when feeling insecure, but if you stand open with your head held high, you will appear much more self-assured.

- If you feel like this isn't working and feels weird, that's okay. Nobody walks with a body part as exaggerated as we want you to do in this exercise, so it should feel awkward and uncomfortable. If no adjectives are coming to mind, that's because you're thinking too much about how strange this feels instead of how you would describe someone who walks like this. Just really commit to it and get rid of all self-judgment, and things should work out.

Continuing The Scene

So we have our emotion, and our partner has theirs, and we started organically. What now? I don't know, why are you asking me!

Kidding...now the fun begins.[21] The play of an improv scene is in how both your emotion, and your partner's emotion interact, and since neither are going to charge them, this journey of two emotions interacting is a lot of fun, so we also want to be aware of how the other person is feeling too. It's not only about you, but them too- that's how we have good chemistry. Whether both of these emotions are different or similar, their interaction – like a scientist mixing two chemicals- is where the exploration and uniqueness happen. One person upset with someone excited, or one person grandiose with someone meek, the combinations are endless!

In real-life, every interaction also has two emotions mixing together, but most of the time, we aren't aware of anyone's emotions but ourselves. Improv teaches us that everything we need comes from listening, so

---

[21] Hopefully you've been having fun this entire time though

listening and assuming what another person's emotion is will help us navigate the improv situation much better. In improv, we want to think how we can use our emotion to bring out more of the emotion of our partner and in life we may use the other person's emotion to navigate the conversation easier. For example:

> PERSON 1 (jolly): *Hello, do you know what aisle the sparkling water is on?*
> PERSON 2 (annoyed): *Maybe aisle seven.*

Now...most of the time, we'd instantly react to something like this, matching their emotion and becoming annoyed back to them.

> PERSON 1 (now annoyed): *What do you mean, maybe? Don't you work here?*

And a nice little argument will ensue, and we're still not any closer to finding that sparkling water. But, since we learned to hold onto our emotions, then we learned to charge that instinctual habit of letting other people's feelings affect us too. If someone is annoyed and you are jolly, just keep being jolly! This trips people up a lot in presentations too. We may go in feeling confident, but as soon as someone who may sound more confident or assured than us asks a question, we fall back into being nervous.

By listening, we want to be aware that other people have emotions that may not match ours. That way, when they respond to us a certain way, it doesn't trip us up. Instead, we start to think "Oh, this person is annoyed. That's interesting. But I'm still going to be jolly 'ol me." Improv teaches us to hold our emotions in scenes no matter what, so when real-life stuff like this happens, we can power through and not let it affect us!

EXERCISE: Count to 100

Here's a good exercise to express different emotions while talking. But what helps here is you don't have to wonder what to say to do it.

The **goal** is to not change the story or WHAT you are saying, but HOW you are saying it and thus expressing more emotions than you normally would be able to.

IMPROV EXERCISE
100 COUNT

Skills Used:
Emotions & Quick-Thinking

1 Make a list of different, random adjectives and emotions.

2 Choose one emotion and start counting from 1 to 100 speaking those numbers using that emotion.

3 After a few numbers, choose a different emotion and use that to say more of the numbers

4 Continue until you've gone up to 100...or until you count to 1,746,294,647- it doesn't have to stop if you're having fun!

5 ADVANCED VERSION: Start telling a true or made-up story, changing your emotions throughout the story.

Why

But that's not all. No, for a limited time, your scene may go well with only using the above techniques, but there's more! Act now, and you'll also want to add in the *why*.

In improv, the *why* is the question of why our character is acting the way they are. What led them to being that emotion in the scene? This is a specific moment from their past, a backstory if you will. It could have been either 10 seconds ago or 10 years ago. It doesn't matter when, but something caused them to be this way.

I'm sure you've been in an argument before where a person was upset at you and never said why. Maybe it went something like this:

PERSON 1: *Just tell me why you're so mad!*
PERSON 2: *You know why!*

But you don't. That's a pretty frustrating scenario, so we don't want to recreate it in our improv either. So we have to define a reason why our character is like this. This also works for our real-life situations too.

Using the previous annoyed/jolly example, maybe you are feeling jolly because you just got a new job you've been wanting, or you heard your favorite song playing, or found a $20 bill on your pocket. Knowing why you are your own emotion will help you hold onto it and give you more stuff to do and say while filtering it all through that emotion.

If we go with the new job reason, you could talk about all the facets of this new job- what you're excited about, how long it took to get, etc. etc. etc. You will literally never run out of stuff to say – and that's not even including listening and responding to the other person.

Learning this next bit of information completely changed my outlook on everyday life, so I hope it helps you too. Most of the time, people's emotions have nothing to do with you. For real. If someone replies *annoying* to you in the store, instead of taking it as a personal attack on you, flip your perspective. This person was feeling this way before you ever came in contact with them.

That other person may be annoyed because they had to come in to work on their day off, or maybe they just had to clean up a mess they didn't make, or maybe they didn't get enough sleep because their neighbor was partying deep into the night. There could be an infinite number of reasons, you just happened to get caught up in their emotional wave.

Understanding other people have emotions *and* that their reasons why have nothing to do with you (unless, of course, you directly did something to annoy or hurt them) is so freeing! Instead of getting caught up in their emotion which is unlike yours, we hold onto ours. The interaction can continue by exploring why they feel that way, either assuming in your head or flat out asking them if they're OK. You keep your emotion, they keep theirs, and the interaction continues for as long as it needs to, and you both go on your merry, or annoyed, way.

This can also apply to presentations or meetings. Sure, we can go into them saying we'll pretend to feel confident, but as soon as something comes to trip us up, *woosh*, our confidence flies out the window. That's because we didn't anchor it with our *why*. What makes you feel confident? Yes, we may have just been pretending, but find some specific reason why and it will keep that confidence in place. Is it that you are well prepared for the day, or like your outfit, or had a good breakfast – whatever! Have your *why*.

The reason really doesn't even matter all that much. We just need one. Most beginner improvisers won't give a specific reason, "I'm tired because I didn't get enough sleep" or, "I'm annoyed because things annoy me." That's like giving the definition of a word by using the word in the definition- it ain't gonna help ya. Be clucking specific! Like how I said the word *clucking* instead of another similar word, specify. Being ambiguous won't be enough to anchor and use your why. It needs to have details to it.

But here's the best part, too...it DOES NOT matter what your reason is. So give any SPECIFIC reason and it will add much to your emotion. It can really be anything because #NoWrongAnswerButNoAnswer. For example, try to come up with a reason that doesn't work with the following emotion:

Emotion: Happy

Why: *My house burned down. Great! Now I get a huge insurance check!*

Why: *I'm being mugged. Now I'll have a great story for the office Christmas party!*

Why: *My cat died. Good, he was sick anyway. Now I can get a dog!*

Although those are examples that in real life wouldn't make us happy, it shows us that really any reason why can work with any emotion. So don't worry about picking a good *why*, just have a specific one.

Once you establish your why, something you discovered in the moment or thought about before you go somewhere, you don't just have it and move on. No! It's an integral part of the scene so go deeper with the details. Why are you getting a big insurance check for your house? Why did it burn down? Why are you looking forward to the money? Keep asking why with details while using your emotion to create an interesting and strong foundation for your character at this moment, all while using what the other person says with their emotion to play off of. Now you've got the beginning workings of a good improv scene.[22]

What vs. How

Starting and finding our emotion at the top of the scene is also what I like to call your "Improv Superpower." If you have a clearly defined emotion, which leads to everything you say being filtered through that emotion, then no matter what the other person does or doesn't do won't ruin the scene.

Maybe you've been in a situation where the other person wasn't interested in the meeting (such as a job interview where the interviewer was tired from the day full of talking to people), but if you have your emotion – maybe *confident*, or *fun*, you'll still be able to continue just as strong even if the other person isn't giving you much back-and-forth. This frees us from the complaint, "well, they weren't giving me much to work with." That happens, but it shouldn't stop us from being our best selves. We can still be powerful no matter what the other person says or doesn't.

If you start with an emotion in your head, let's say *excited*, then even if someone else starts with, "Hey, it sure is cold in here," you still get to keep your emotion! Now you can reply excited about the weather. But if you come in thinking, "I'm going to say how much I like their shoes," and the other person speaks first and says, "Hey, it sure is cold in here" and you say, "Wow, I really like your shoes!" Well, you're off to a bad start because you didn't even listen to what the other person just said, and their first impression of you is someone who doesn't listen. Oops! When both people try to force their original ideas in an improv scene, things get messy,

---

[22] Beginning workings because there's more that we'll get into soon.

confusing, and never move forward. But starting with only emotion can fit over any idea the other person brings to the table.

Now, what about if you were the one starting? Can you still come up with a pre-conceived opener? A common misconception on how to start a scene or conversation is that we need to think of *what* to do. "Oh, it'd be funny if I made a joke about the food!" The problem with only having an idea of "what to do" is the idea will dry up very fast if we don't have an emotion behind it. Great, you took the common advice and started with a joke. Now what? Better keep coming up with funny and witty things to say to keep your scene going! But that's not good improv, that's being witty, and having to stand there and quickly come up with funny things to say in the moment is not the easiest thing. In fact, it's very difficult for a lot of people, and I'm trying to teach you easy methods. Otherwise, this book would be all about how to make puns, pop-culture references, and how to do over-used impressions.

Starting with a joke is fine- it relaxes people and tells them we don't take things so seriously. But if we follow up your joke with other boring things, falling back on our default emotion, the situation will be a failure. The point of starting with a joke is to start with the emotion of *humorous*, but most of us don't realize this and drop that emotion. We can really start with anything (we'll get to that), but it's more important *how* we do or say something than *what* we actually do or say. So please have something else besides our one opening line, specifically an emotion behind it. Starting off with only an idea is called premise based improv.

EXERCISE: The Glove

This 'Keith Saltojanes original' exercise is used to show how any emotion at all will always fit over any idea at all.

IMPROV EXERCISE
THE GLOVE

Skills Used:
Emotions, Initiations, Responding

1 Write down a list of emotions, anywhere from 5-10. Then pick one to start with.

2 Get a suggestion of a word and come up with an opening line and idea for a possible conversation.

3 Write what the opening line of the conversation might be.

4 Using the emotion you already picked, write what your response would be below.

5 Now use a different emotion and respond to that same first line. It should be pretty easy and work every time.

The conversation will continue easily from there and it will work every time, which you can prove by choosing another emotion and starting the process over. Even your "hard" emotion will work if you commit to keeping them. The **goal** of this is to demonstrate that even when thinking of an emotion before a suggestion is even taken, that emotion still perfectly interlaces with whatever the idea is.

Group Version:

Do the same thing above, but one person thinks of an emotion (and doesn't tell the other), while the other person thinks of a way to start a scene and does. Then continue the back-and-forth using your emotion. It can end after a minute or so, but you'll see how you can easily keep going.

Advanced Version:

Something else that's fun to experiment with using this exercise is for both people to come up with their own individual premises and not have any emotion before the scene begins (for the purposes of this experiment, it is the only time you are allowed to not have emotion in a scene). Then using that idea, and without dropping what each wants the scene to be about, attempt to do a scene. Nine times out of ten, the conversation will end up being an argument where both people are trying to figure out what the scene's about.

This shows that if you start a scene or conversation with a pre-laid out idea only and no emotion, you have a higher risk of the situation faltering from the beginning. Start with emotions, not with ideas, and react in the moment.

Tips:

- Definitely don't change your emotion after the scene is initiated, thinking that your emotion won't work. The whole purpose of this exercise is to show you that any emotion will work with any idea.

Premise-Based vs. Organic-Based

There are two types of long-form improv and two ways to start a scene. Premise-based and Organic-based. Premise-based simply means we start and initiate a scene with a clear idea in mind (premise) that we communicate to the other person. Here are some examples:

> PERSON: *Finally, I can eat my dinner in peace, and no one is going to interrupt me.*
> (which is inviting people to interrupt them in the scene)
> PERSON: *Hey, Local firefighters, let's talk about why all these buildings keep burning down.*
> (signaling the other improvisers to come in and be bad firefighters)
>
> PERSON: *Now I know you keep sneezing, but please give me my results, Doctor.*
> (telling the scene partner to be the Doctor and that they will keep sneezing)

Premise-based improv is all about coming up with funny ideas from either the suggestion or other scenes right away. The ideas aren't thought of the day before and brought to the improv show. They are still improv, just from the side before the performer steps on stage.

The pros of premise-based improv are that it gets to what our idea was very quickly, has less room for error in getting our point across - since we're telling the other person exactly what we want the scene to be about, and they are usually funnier, faster since, again, we are getting right to the idea.

The cons of premise improv is that if we don't have an idea, we won't be able to do a scene. If our mind goes blank or we're having an off-day, the thought of starting a scene or conversation from a vast space of empty nothingness will be very hard. Scenes that start from that place usually tentatively begin with an "Oh, hi.... what are you doing..." or some other sort of non-specific statement or question. Even if you have a few premises you can pull, usually, after 5-10 minutes, the well goes dry.

While Premise based improv is another great skill to learn, not having a scene idea shouldn't stop us from improvising. This brings us to... Organic-based improv.

Organic improv literally means we don't have a full idea/premise for a scene and start naturally. This can be anything from a body posture, move-ment, sound, or a line without a full premise, such as, "Bartender, I'll take another drink." Or, "I'd like to look at the puppies that are up for adoption." Or, "Get on the bus. We leave in one minute."

These are all just sparks of ideas, not fully thought out premises. We aren't sure where the scene will go, and we'll build it, in the moment, with the other person.

The pros of organic-based scenes are that we can improvise at any time with any smidgen of an idea or even none. We can do anything, find our emotion, and start a conversation there. It's very freeing to let go and trust the process into making a good improv scene. It took me six long years of improv to be able to do this, and it was the greatest, and best, hurdle to overcome for me. To just trust you'll be to make something out of nothing is great, and what true improvisation is.

There are cons to organic-based, and that is if we kind of know where we want the scene to go, and don't communicate that with the other person, our idea may be changed into another idea altogether. Then, sometimes, the reaction is to force our idea to work with the already established idea, which is wrong and will cause us to not listen and build off of what they are saying. Drop your other idea and work with what's in front of you. Just because it's organic doesn't mean you don't make a choice. Still, make a strong choice (emotion) and stick with it. No matter the improv style, we still want it to move the conversation or scene forward.

Learn both styles. They both come in handy. Outside of improv, being able to start a conversation at any time, or respond to one that someone starts with you, is very helpful. Sometimes we don't know we're about to be in an improv situation, and that's where organic-improv skills can help. But other times, we know we will be in one (such as a presentation or interview), and that's a good place to use premise-based. [23]

Be Aware

Emotions are the greatest thing to have when improvising; it comes down to self-awareness. Being in the moment, knowing how you feel, and how the other person feels will allow you to react and navigate any situation instead of just being on auto pilot based on many of our past experiences with people and not truly deciding how to react. Know your emotion, hold onto it, listen to the other person, and thus, have better scenes...in life.

EXERCISE: Good, Bad, & Worst Advice

This short form improv game can be played with group participation if desired.

Before the exercise begins, begins three people will be designated as advice givers, one being someone who gives good advice, one who gives bad advice, and one who gives the absolute worst advice one could give – each of these should be played with matching emotions too (for example, a good advice giver may be *excited*, while the bad could be *depressed*.)

Next, the Leader will get someone from the group who needs advice on something in their life (it could be for a real problem or a made-up one if no one wants to share their personal drama in public). That volunteer says

---

[23] See chapter called Long Form for more

their issue, and the three people proceed to advise on it and will give their advice in the order of Good, Bad, and Worst.

GOOD, BAD, WORST ADVICE

Skills Used: Emotions + Creativity + Idea Generation

HOW TO DO IT

1. Think of something that someone may need advice on *(such as moving, changing jobs, having kids, what to wear, anything!)*

GOOD ADVICE

2. Legitimately try to give some good advice on the problem- actually trying to be helpful here.

BAD ADVICE

3. Think of bad advice about the issue - advice that probably isn't something you should normally do.

WORST ADVICE

4. Give the most terrible, wretchedest advice that anyone could give for that situation. Truly the worst advice they can come up with here.

GOAL

5. Work on creating different thoughts and ideas for the same starting point using specific emotions *(here being good, bad, or worst)* in a fun improv game

Good, Bad, Worst Advice Example:

Advice on "My neighbor has annoying loud parties every weekend."

> GOOD ADVICE: *Go over to their house during the week with a plate of cookies and tell them how it's disruptive to your weekend, and if they can keep the noise down a little bit.*

> BAD ADVICE: *Wait for it to happen again and yell out your window for them to turn it down, getting angrier each time.*

> WORST ADVICE: *Go get a very expensive, powerful sound system-such as one that a concert venue uses. Pay someone to set it all up with the speakers all facing your neighbor's house. Next, spend all week making a playlist of the most annoying terrible music you can illegally download. Then, when that party starts, blast the music so loud that you all lose your hearing. Problem. Solved.*

The **goal** here is to work on creating different thoughts and ideas through a specific emotion, of which is good, bad, or worst.

Solo Version:

If you want to do this exercise on your own, you can just play each of the three parts and respond to a list of random questions or issues that someone might have. Do it a few times to really get used to thinking of made-up advice quicker each time, all while expressing different emotions.

CHAPTER 5
THE FOUR PILLARS
OF A SCENE

Now that we have our emotions/character and we found out why we are that way in a scene, we can continue a scene pretty well... for a bit. But there is something else to add, to make our scenes, and improv scenarios for that matter, unstoppable. It's what I call the Four Pillars of an Improv Scene. And instead of making you wait to find out what they are, I'm going to tell you right now. Without any further delay, here they are. Because why would you be reading this if you didn't want to know what they were? So I should just tell you already, you know? Are you ready? I don't want it to drag on and on anymore. Here we go...for real...

The Four Pillars are your *Character, Relationship, Environment,* and *Why;* or the acronym C.R.E.W. Having all of your C.R.E.W. in a scene will allow your scene to go on, literally forever. I compare these four things to the legs of a table. If you have all four, the table is sturdy. It can hold things on it all day long. But it's a bit wobbly if it's missing one leg while it still works. Missing two, it will be very unstable. And only having one leg isn't quite a good table at all.

The same for our scenes. If we only have our Character, their scene will be rocky. Only having Environment and Relationship, better, but still uneven. We want to have them all have the best improv scene possible.

So let's go over them now. First, we'll talk about what they are, and then go into how to use them. Now I present your table:

Character

In the scene, your character is who you are pretending to be or acting as. We talked about this a lot in the previous chapter when it comes to your emotion, but it's more than that. It's also who you are and what you do. For example, you are sad, angry, hungry- whatever emotion- but you are also a lawyer, doctor, telemarketer, nun, dad, etc. Any combination of emotions/adjectives and who the person can be is acceptable. So they aren't just a Doctor, but a Sad Doctor, or a Hungry Lawyer, or an Angry Nun. I'm sure you're already thinking of all of these comedic possibilities, and that's the point. Have your emotion/adjective, but also has who this person is.

Outside of performing improv, your Character is your emotion at this moment and also who you are. You may be a Caring Mom at home, but in this courtroom, you're a Focused Lawyer. We know who we are, for the most part, but how often are we aware of it in the moment? Sure, I'm Keith who is writing this book, but how do I feel right now, and what version of Keith am I? Again, be present and aware and listen, even to yourself.

Relationship

This is how these two people know each other. Being strangers in a scene doesn't help anything, because most likely, the scene will be all about questions, which doesn't move the scene forward at all. Chances are the two people will just be asking, "Where are you going? What do you do for work?" Etc. etc. That helps nothing. Knowing the other character in the scene will allow you to assume all that information and get to the more interesting and fun parts of the scene.

In real life, we are in a relationship with everyone we meet all day long. As soon as we interact with someone, we're in a relationship. Obviously, there are siblings, friends, co-worker, etc. relationships, but even beyond that, they exist. Maybe you are two people at a bank, or two people at a stop sign. Even in a real-life-strangers scenario, where we do indeed interact with strangers, we can go deeper. Where did you meet? Do they always go this way (if at a train or a grocery store)? What do you have in common? Do they know a lot about you and have been stalking you online? All of these details are found within the relationship. Then the mixing in of your Characters will make the interaction even more fun. One person is jealous of the other, while the other is in love with them. You get it. Have a relationship in your scenes and notice them in real life. It is one of the pillars, after all.

Environment

This means WHERE the scene is taking place. There is never a time in life where we are just standing, facing someone in no specific location, and yet there are so many improv scenes like this. Usually, it's because we are still too up in our heads to even take what could be around us. Are you at a community pool, a coffee shop by your old college, the back of a pickup truck, or hiding under the desk in the Mayor's office? We want to have a specific location. At Disneyland? Where in Disneyland? These details will add to the scene. A scene between two old friends in a park is a lot different than one in a dumpster.

This also applies to us in life. Yes, we're at the office, but where we are specifically will affect us depending on the location.

There are two ways we can use the environment as well. One is to physically interact with the objects in the space. For example, making eggs in a kitchen, or organizing papers in a tax office.

The second way to use the environment is to see it and feel it. For example, your character is "feeling cold" in a location that is chilly Notice what's around you in the pretend environment, and use it to further your scene. Everything around us and said and done is available to further build the situation we are in. Take nothing for granted!

Why

The final Pillar of an Improv scene is the Why. We discussed this earlier as in 'Why is your character's emotion the way it is?' but this fourth Pillar also means 'Why is this particular scene happening? Why is this going on? And Why should anyone care to watch it?'

Improv scenes are about people dealing with problems, not solving them. They are about days that break the normal routine of that person's routine. A scene that goes like:

> PERSON 1: *Honey, time to go to school.*
> PERSON 2: *Ok, Grams, I'm ready, and I won't be late.*

...is pretty boring. Something else better happen in this scene, but who wants to watch this on stage? Not me, I know that. Something has to happen. Maybe something like this:

> PERSON 1: *Honey, time to go to school.*
> PERSON 2: *No, Grams, today I'm not going to school. You're going to teach me instead!*

Now, this breaks the normal routine and is far more interesting. Sure, it may sound like a denial, but again, it's the characters disagreeing, not the performers. They agree to the situation and can go from there.

This is also how every movie and TV begins, also called the inciting incident. We get introduced to the characters and then, something happens that they have to deal with, and then we watch them deal with it for the remainder of the film or series.

Outside of improv scenes, we want our Why in life too. Having a conversation that asks a bunch of questions of the other person (shame on you breaking that rule!) and that's very surface level is also boring. Instead, why are you in this interaction? Is it to make new friends? Then go in with that focus and make the interaction about that. Find common ground or create inside jokes. A conversation between your mechanic and your boss is very different, so you should be aware of your Why to be able to navigate it better.

Ask yourself why this is happening, how it breaks the mold of everyday life, and why anyone should care. If, in the school example, the Mom didn't care about him missing school, that's also boring. Give any and every idea some weight of importance, and your interaction, and scene, will be way more interesting.

EXERCISE: Four Line Scenes

This exercise will help you establish your CREW as quickly as possible so you can familiarize yourself with it in conversations.

FOUR LINE SCENES

SKILLS USED: CREW + CONVERSATIONS

1 **HOW TO DO IT**
Get a suggestion for a topic of conversation or situation. Don't try to think of an easy one, as random as the suggestion can be, the better!

2 **ACT IT OUT**
Do a short act-out in which you speak both sides of the conversation, saying only two lines each.

3 **ESTABLISH CREW**
Within these four lines establish the characters, relationship, environment, and why of the scenario.

4 **WHAT NEXT**
Knowing the CREW, think about what could happen next if the situation was to continue with what's already been set-up.

GOAL: Notice and establish CREW because once you have it, CREW gives you everything you need to keep going.

Four Line Scene Example:

PERSON ONE: *Hi Dad, I'm home from school.*
PERSON TWO: *Great, I've been excited all day for you to get home because I made us our favorite dinner!*
PERSON ONE: *Well, let me wash my hands and sit right down at this table to eat because I'm hungry.*
PERSON TWO: *I'll heat it up, and then it's piles and piles of roasted onions for us!*

So we know that it's a Dad (who is excited) and Son (who is hungry), in their home kitchen, and they are going to eat their favorite, yet weird, dinner.

Remember, CREW gives you the roadmap to your scene. Everything you need to know to continue is within that CREW. Talking out loud afterward uses the brain-muscle to create it without the pressure of having to do the scene itself. The **goal** is to be aware of that CREW and establish it as quickly as possible.

You don't have to find your CREW within four lines when you aren't doing this exercise. The sooner it's known, the easier the scene will be, but you can take your time normally. We still want that Emotion as soon as possible, but for the focus of this exercise, we are just getting used to having CREW at the top. Many scenes start and continue, and both people aren't conscious of their CREW, which is why most scenes fail.

Tips:

- -If you happen to establish your CREW in under four lines, you can just keep the scene going until four lines are completed. Nice job, you overachiever.
- It's good to take your time with each line, and be aware that what you are saying will be adding to the goal of the exercise, which is to find your CREW in four lines only.

- Use this during your conversation to keep them from getting dried up and boring.
- This might be clunky and awkward because of how slow you could be speaking, but that's the point. We want you to be conscious of your improv moves instead of just saying something and not knowing why you said it. Awareness of being in the moment and listening (first rule!) will give you better success than just randomly doing stuff hoping it's funny.

How to Use CREW

Now that we have established our CREW, it's not time to move on and talk about something else. No, silly. It's time to use the pieces of CREW to add details and play within the created realms.

Let's use an example of an improv scene where two brothers have to fix a car. We wouldn't just just say, "Hand me the wrench, I'll fix this," and be done. But instead, we expand upon each of these Pillars, moving back and forth between them and never running out of stuff to talk about.

Since in this scene the relationship is between two brothers, then we can assume all the information that comes with these people having a past together and talk about that during your scene. Things like:

PERSON 1: *This is just like when you broke my Lego castle when I was eight.*
PERSON 2: *I don't know how to fix it. You were always the handy one. Dad liked you more because of it.*

PERSON 1: *Well, here we are again, having to work together. I said I'd never do that again.*

All of this will express their Characters, in which we can explore that emotion and who they are more. We also want to do this with the other Pillars too. Here are more examples:

Using Environment:

PERSON 1: *We're in the middle of the desert. There's not going to be anyone coming by to help us anytime soon.*
PERSON 2: *Look, it's getting dark. There's nothing we can do now but set up some shelter for the night.*
PERSON 1: *Do you have any water in your car? It's 100 degrees out here!*

Using Why:

PERSON 1: *We need to get this fixed asap or we're going to be late for Mom's funeral.*
PERSON 2: *I told you we should have rented a car. You never listen to my advice just because I'm younger.*
(also has a relationship)

PERSON 1: *The zombies are going to catch us. Hurry up and let's fix this thing!*

And we talked about characters/emotion earlier and can use that too. Use these specifics to add information and details to your scene so we can, and better, go deeper while progressing the scene.

In life, we know our CREW too. You know how you feel each day, how you relate to people around you, where you live, and why you are doing the things you go and do each day. If you know the answers to all of these things, then you probably have a pretty stable life. It's the times when we are missing a Pillar, that things feel off. For example:

Missing Character: *I don't know who I am yet.*
Missing Relationship: *I don't know how I feel towards this other person.*
Missing Why: *I just don't know why I took this job in the first place..*

These are the great questions of living our life, and we don't run out of Environment in our life. It's always there. It's only how much we notice it, take it in, and use to react to.

You can use CREW in every situation you're in during your real life too. For example, in a conversation, instead of not knowing what to talk about, use each Pillar as a jumping off point.

— Talk about how you or the other person feels *(Character)*
— Exchange views on Why they feel that way *(Character)*
— Talk about what they do and why *(Character)*
— Discuss how you know each other and your memories together, even if only from a few minutes ago or in a pretend future *(Relationship)*
— Talk about the location you are in. What's interesting about it? *(Environment)*
— Consider the reason why you are both in this conversation at this moment *(Why)*

Then just weave in and out and back and forth, going farther with more specifics and information within these Pillars and then tell me you don't have stuff to discuss. We don't run out of things to do in our overall life, so you shouldn't run out of things to say in a 3-minute improv conversation either. With the four legs, you can literally continue forever – but please don't. We all want to interact with more people too.

EXERCISE: Locked Up

This exercise forces us to stay "Locked Up" within the constraints of a single Pillar at a time while having a one-sided conversation and also shows us that when we do, we can explore a lot.

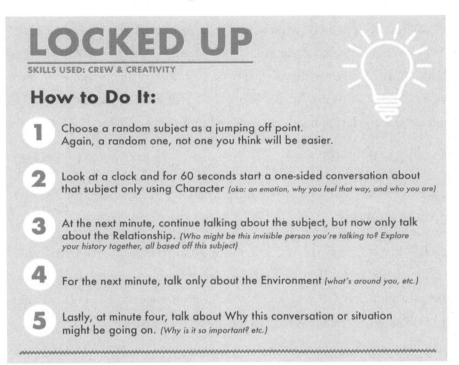

LOCKED UP

SKILLS USED: CREW & CREATIVITY

How to Do It:

1 Choose a random subject as a jumping off point. Again, a random one, not one you think will be easier.

2 Look at a clock and for 60 seconds start a one-sided conversation about that subject only using Character *(aka: an emotion, why you feel that way, and who you are)*

3 At the next minute, continue talking about the subject, but now only talk about the Relationship. *(Who might be this invisible person you're talking to? Explore your history together, all based off this subject)*

4 For the next minute, talk only about the Environment *(what's around you, etc.)*

5 Lastly, at minute four, talk about Why this conversation or situation might be going on. *(Why is it so important? etc.)*

Our **goal** with this one is to force you to squeeze out information from each Pillar instead of only touching the surface and moving on to the next thing. Try doing it again with longer "Locked Up" times or even going back to the first Pillar once you finish the Why section.

Tips:

- You can also do this with another person, and both of you are "Locked Up" in that Pillar until the time ends.

CREW vs. Who, What, Where

CREW is my version of what's more commonly taught in improv as the "Who, What, Where" meaning, "Who are these people? What are they doing? And Where are they." The issue I have with that is that even once we establish our Who, What, Where, we still have to develop more to make the scene last. There's no usage of Emotions or Why. For Example:

PERSON 1: *We are friends (who) fishing (what) in a lake (where).*

Ok, now what? If that's all we have, then we better make things more interesting quickly.

CREW just breaks it down a little more, giving us specific roads to follow with each Pillar. So if you're ever talking to someone who does improv and you mention CREW, the blank look on their face is because they know it as Who, What, Where. Basically the same idea.[24]

Boring Scenes

There are two types of scenes in improv that are basically blacklisted, that you're never supposed to do because they are too boring.

Teaching Scenes

A teaching scene, in which one character is teaching another character how to do something, is one scene we're "never supposed to do" in improv.

---

[24] CREW is also a spinoff of the idea of CROW created by Keith Johnstone. What can we say, great Keiths think alike?

Usually, these types of scenes don't work out because one person is leading the scene while the other follows. For example:

> PERSON 1: *How do you do them dance moves? Can you teach them to me?*
> PERSON 2: *You do it like this. No, not like that... like this.*

This scene breaks the rules of improv for a couple of reasons. One, the first person is not *assuming* to know what's going on, and they're *asking* the other person to show them something, which outside of the scene does not exist. The other person then has to make it up on the spot even though neither of them know more than the other.

Two, the second person denies what the first is doing and tells them how to do something in the scene. It would be the equivalent of a scene going like this:

> PERSON 1: *Hi Dad. I'm home from school.*
> PERSON 2: *No, you're not, you're my husband, and you're a police officer.*

Bad improv! Most of the time, scenes like this happen because one person is a little too nervous about making a decision, so they lean on the other person to make all the decisions and just follow them. Boring, and doesn't make us better at improv.

So should we never do teaching scenes? Teaching happens in real life, and if everything in an improv scene is supposed to mirror what can happen in real life, then that would mean teaching scenes should work. But how? Glad you asked because I'm going to tell you!

Teaching scenes really don't work because it's all about *what's* happening in the scene. There's no emotion, and we don't know why this is such a big deal (outside of the big dance contest coming up, which is usually the reason someone panicky pulls out of nowhere). Now it's that same scene happen where there was a relationship and emotions, a teaching scene could work.

> PERSON 1 (excited): *How do you do those dance moves, like this?*
> PERSON 2 (strict): *Listen, if you want to get this scholarship, you're going to have to work harder! I need you here every day at 5am and we'll practice until your feet blister, and then we'll practice some more!*

See, now there's some legs for this scene to stand on and it's interesting instead of just one person following another, and we don't know why. So the same things in our daily life, if we're just leading someone else, and there's not an equal back-and-forth with Emotions, and Why this is going on, it's going to be a pretty painful conversation to endure...for both parties involved.

Transaction Scenes

The other "forbidden scene" is the transaction scene, in which one character purchases an item from another. Here's an example of how they usually go

> PERSON 1: *Hey, how much for that Bagel?*
> PERSON 2: *Two dollars.*
> PERSON 1: *Okay, here's $2.*
> PERSON 2: *Here is your bagel. Thank you. Have a good day. Bye.*

Woof...talk about boring. Again, there's no emotion, and no stakes as to why the situation is taking place, so who cares? But again, transactions happen in real life, so they don't work in improv? You guessed it- have emotions and have a reason why this is taking place.

> PERSON 1 (nervous): *Um, ex-excuse me. How much for that Bagel?*
> PERSON 2 (confident): *Two dollars.*

Person 1 pulls a bunch of trading cards from their pocket)

PERSON 1 (nervous): *Look, I don't have much money and just need some food. So can I trade you this old Topps baseball card for an Everything?*

PERSON 2 (confident): *Ha, I mean, I can tell that card is worth $500 so yeah, I'll trade it and pay for the bagel myself.*

With these additions got something interesting going, and within a forbidden transaction scene! There's emotion, and there are stakes...which we've been saying a lot. If you have emotions and why, any situation works, in real life and in improv. So if you are ever in an improv class and someone says there's something you can't do, ask why and figure out how to do it successfully.[25]

That's about it for this chapter. Find your CREW, use it further in the scenario, and if you ever get lost along the way, just go back to a piece of CREW and hunker down in it and build more.

---

[25] A lot of improv that I learned was taught using these older rules, such as Who, What, Where. After doing a bad scene, teachers would say what we did wrong, but after a good scene, they would never break down why that worked. It's just as important to know why something works as it is to why it sucked. There is no mystery, there are practical skills, which you are reading now.

EXERCISE: Silent Dialogue

Skills Used:

* Quick-Thinking
* Creativity
* Scenes and Conversations

Don't you have access to a group of people to practice your full improv conversations with all the time? No problem. This exercise is perfect for strengthening that muscle.

IMPROV EXERCISE

SILENT DIALOGUE

How to Do It:

01 Turn on any TV or movie and mute the volume. A program that you are less familiar with is more helpful here.

02 Start to make up the dialogue between the characters on screen. Say them out loud and quickly switch to the other person as soon as they begin speaking.

Focus on the **goal** of building good conversations that can continue for a while. It's great to do this for an entire half-hour show as each character will be revisited and can continue the conversation where they left off last time. This is a great way to keep you on your feet, especially because you don't know when the actors' mouths will be moving or when the scene changes. Again, there is no right or wrong answer, so if it doesn't match their real words- totally fine!

Tips:

- It's also fun to do this with another person, and each of you assign yourselves to one of the characters on screen. If you've ever seen Mystery Science Theater 3000 (or any of its offshoots) they sometimes do the same thing and it's always a blast!
- Because the actors on screen aren't listening to what you're saying, you will probably be cut off in each sentence you're conveying. That's okay. It just works on keeping you quick on your feet even more.

CHAPTER 6

INITIATIONS: PART 1

The method used to start a scene in improv is called "Initiation." It's the first moment of a scene, the first spark that the rest of the scene will grow from and the same applies to initiating any communication in your everyday life.

So how do you initiate? Do anything at all. End of chapter. Bye.

CHAPTER 7

INITIATIONS: PART 2

O k, but really, that was a joke- sort of. You really can make an initiation by doing anything at all. In improv, it's called making a strong, bold, or big choice at the start,[26] which all really means don't be unsure, ambiguous, or unclear. Do something *specific* – there's that word again. I've seen so many boring improv scenes where people remain unsure, middle-of-the-road participants, waiting for the scene to come to them. It's way more fun to watch, be in a scene with someone, or be the one doing it, to make a choice and do something clear at the top of the scene. It can be anything, but it has to be *something*. Really, literally, I truly mean do *anything,* and that can work as your initiation.

Can I scream? Yes.

Can I do jumping jacks? Yep.

Can I walk out there and stare blankly at the audience? Absolutely.

You can even go into a scenario thinking you're going to do one thing, but suddenly trip and fall flat on your face. *That* is then your initiation. Once something happens, your initiation has been done, and things are underway. You just have to make it happen.

Starting with a "Hey..." or just standing next to someone with nothing to say, doing nothing isn't an initiation, though- because you haven't done

---

[26] "Big" refers to size but is commonly used as a direction note. It means adds energy and clarity. Be precise.

anything. Sure, saying "hey" is something, but it's still ambiguous. What do you mean "Hey?" Doing anything means initiating with specificity and clarity, so there are tiny sparks in what you did that can ignite the rest of the interaction. So do anything...specific.

But...since *anything* is infinite and doesn't actually help us with how to start, let's break it down and give us something more to work with. Usually, when our options are unlimited, it's harder to think of something.

So here are six easy ways, in no particular order, that we can organically initiate.[27] We start with:

1) Emotion
2) Posture
3) Word
4) Sound
5) Physical Action
6) CREW

1. Emotion

You are probably so over me talking about emotions. Like, how many chapters is this going to go on? Well, all of them, maybe. Emotions are helpful from the moment we first learn them all the way through, however long you are going to be put in improv situations, so forever.

In improv, starting with an emotion is the only pre-conceived idea you can have that will work with whatever your partner does (remember that Glove exercise?). Initiating a scene from an emotional place is a great way to start and you can do this in your interpersonal communication situations too. Emotions give you a clear way of being and allows you to come from

---

[27] Organically. You can still start with an pre-planned idea as we talked about with Premise-based improv. But this is for when you have no ideas at all.

a place where everything else will be filtered through the way you are feeling. See that chapter on Emotions if you need a reminder of how to do this. You know what? Read that one again anyway, since Emotions are so important!

2. Posture

Initiating an improv scene starting from a posture is another great method. This simply means standing a different way than you normally do and reacting to it. We assume who this person is from their physical appearance and go from there. Alternatively, your partner can react off of how you're standing. If you have your hands on your hips, you're probably upset with the other person in your scene. If you are laying stretched out across some chairs, you're probably lazy.

In life, changing our posture also gives us a jumping off point. If we stand head held high and shoulders back, we instantly feel more aware and more confident- instead of head down and a closed off body posture. Whatever your body positioning is, it's the first spark to lead you to the rest of your interaction. Stand differently than you normally do; strike a pose. There's nothing to it.[28]

3. Word

Starting with a word simply means to say a word, any word and go from there. "Butterflies", "Waterpark" or "Grilled Tofu." Whatever the word is, it's a spark that can lead us to the next place. But what word do you say? Again, doesn't matter!

In improv, we could just use the suggestion that was given by the audience as the word. That's the simplest way to start. If the suggestion is *Technology*,

---

[28] Please note: this reference to a Madonna song was already outdated when I wrote it. Thank you.

say that actual word. And in life, when people aren't suggesting what to start with, you can use what's around you, which is basically like one big, breathing, alive suggestion. See a cat outside? Starts with the word *cat*. The point here is that saying something will allow your mind to connect to something else and thus allow you to think of what to say next. Check out these examples:

> PERSON: *Butterflies...we're all just like butterflies, who have changed from how were once were.*
> (maybe this turns out to be people talking about growing up.)
> PERSON: *Water park...that's where I want to go for my birthday.*
> (maybe a family making plans)
> PERSON: *Grilled chicken...you're so afraid to give that speech you're not just chicken, but grilled chicken!*
> (maybe about two people at a wedding)
> PERSON: *Technology...that's what today's lecture is about.*
> (maybe a professor teaching a college course)

All of these examples work for the start of an improv scene, but also work for initiating a conversation with anyone in life too. Ok, maybe not the technology example...unless you are a professor who wasn't sure what your lecture would be that day- then it does, and you're welcome!

The point is that we normally overthink everything and pre-plan entire sentences before we ever say them. And since our brain isn't the mode in which communication happens (our mouths or hands are), usually something thought up completely in our heads comes out differently anyway. So instead of waiting until you have "the perfect line," say a word. It really doesn't matter what you say to start or what you follow it up with, but it's something, and something will lead you to more something, and thus an interaction happening

4. Sound

Similar to starting with a random word, we can also initiate a scene with a sound. A scream, a yawn, a groan, etc., will lead us to something else.

> PERSON: *(yawns)... oh wow, I haven't had coffee in hours, and I usually drink 7 cups a day.*

I don't think I need to reiterate this again, but I will, again, it doesn't matter what the sound is. Just make it and justify why you did it. Just fill in why you made the sound you did, and your interaction is off to the races.[29]

5. Physical Action

This is a common yet very effective, way to begin an improv scene. Before you say anything at all, you begin with action. This goes back hand-in-hand[30] with using your Environment.

If the improv suggestion is "Swimming Pool" and someone begins by miming that they are holding a garden hose that is filling the imaginary pool with water, they not only have initiated their scene but also have your first clue into where it's taking place.

Luckily in real life, we know where we are at all times, unlike the invisible environment that comes from improvising on stage. A physical action means to interact with that environment. Start by raising your glass, making a grandiose gesture towards something or someone, or turning your chair around to sit on it like a cool kid...yet again, it doesn't matter what you do as long as it's specific.

---

[29] Which makes complete sense if you started with the sound of a bugle.

[30] Pun *so* intended

Think about all the items we interact with throughout our day: phones, brushing our teeth, making breakfast, driving to work, writing a "Hey Boss, shove it, I quit" note- we do a lot of physical actions without even thinking about them throughout the day, so being aware of these is another wonderful way to initiate.

And, I'm getting tired of saying it, but you can do anything, it matters not what you do. You can use an action related to where you are (such as raising a glass), but you don't have to. You could also put the glass on your head and walk like a penguin- hey, it's you that has to follow-up with what comes next, so have at it. Just do something.

6. CREW

Lastly, we can use any of the elements of CREW for our initiation simply by connecting the situations to it. We can start with our character/ emotion in this moment, how we relate to another person, talk about something in the environment, or why we're both at this location here and now. So. Many. Options!

Examples:

To hit home how these six techniques work even more, I'll now give some examples. Pretending we were at a Baseball game and you wanted to initiate a conversation with someone:

1. Emotion: If baseball fills you with excitement, be excited. If you have no opinion on baseball, be detached.

> PERSON: (excited) *It's really exciting to see these players doing the thing they love most.*
> PERSON: (aloof) It *seems pointless that they try to hit the ball only to run and come back to where they started.*

2. <u>Posture</u>: Start with your arms up like you're trying to catch a fly ball. The conversation doesn't have to be only about a fly ball. It's just a starting point.

> PERSON: (arms up) *I'm ready. If a fly ball comes my way, I'm going to be the first to get it. You ever catch one?*

3. <u>Word</u>: Saying the literal word "Baseball" could lead to something unique.

> PERSON: *Baseball! Baseball! ...people shout things out all the time... hitter, pitcher...but no one ever just says the name of the game.*

4. <u>Sound</u>: Making a clicking sound as if a bat just hit a baseball could lead to something as well.

> PERSON: (clicking sound) *I like to make the sound of a baseball being hit to try to fool the players that another game is going on nearby and causing them FOMO.*

5. <u>Physical Action</u>: Tossing invisible peanuts in the air and trying to catch them in your mouth.

> PERSON: (doing that action) *I like the practice with no peanuts first before I spend the money on the actual thing.*

6. <u>CREW</u>:

Character: pretending you are an umpire while ordering a hot dog.

Relationship: both people are fellow fans, so you could talk about when you got your first souvenir of the team.

Environment: any interaction with the chairs, the fold up, or the stairs, or how it's loud there and hard to have a conversation.

Why: What brought you to the game? Was it someone else's idea or the actual travel means that brought you to the game?

There you have it, six random examples I improvised just now. Am I going to go back and change them after more thought? No. Because I want to walk the walk- or at least write and show you that they can be anything, even if you could have thought of better ways to start after the fact. Just do something specific and go from there.

So try using these six ways to start your next six interactions. You'll see that you'll never need an idea ever again and can start a conversation at any time.

EXERCISE: Initiation List

Practicing initiations alone is possible, which will get you more used to it when you have to start conversing in the real world.

INITIATION LIST

SKILLS USED: Starting conversations + Building Ideas

1 **HOW TO DO IT**
Make a list of ten random words

2 **WRITE DOWN**
Six ways that you could initiate from them using the method that we just learned

3 **GET UP**
With your list, try getting up and initiating the ideas as if you were starting a conversation with someone, going through all your initiations you wrote down.

GOAL: Starting exchanges in a non-stressful situation so it will be easier when that time comes (such as a networking event or meeting)

Initiation List Example: Trains

1) Emotion: Tired (if trains make you tired)
2) Posture: Head bobbing to the side as you fight the urge to fall asleep
3) Word: Train... (which could lead you to even talking about training pets)
4) Sound: Woooowooo (such as the sound of a train, but can be used for excitement in your scenario)
5) Physical Action: Someone pulling the cord that makes the train make the above sound, which looks a lot like pumping your first in excitement
6) CREW: C- a character who has all the power like a train conductor; R- fellow passengers whom you sit next to for your journey, E- the luggage shelf above your seat; W- on this train to go visit a friend and it's more fun than taking a plane

Starting exchanges seems like a daunting task, but the more you practice it when you are not in a stressful situation (like a networking event or meeting), the easier it will be to do when that time comes, and that's the **goal** with this exercise.

What if Someone Else Starts?

Wait, wait, wait... we can initiate the interaction first, but what if someone beats us to it? In improv, like in real life, most people don't like starting, but it does happen. Then what do we do? Should we just talk over them with our own creative initiation, right? No. Please never do that unless you want to be known as 'that person" whom no one likes having conversations with.

Just as we went through techniques on how to start, there are also certain ways to respond when someone else initiates before you. When this happens, it usually means they have some idea of what to talk about, which makes your job even easier. *But* it could also mean that they just had a strong initiation (good for them) and nothing else to follow-up with... which is also fine because you both can build it together in what's called.... *improv.*

Since improv is really just listening and reacting, then do that, and you'll be good.

Here are the three specific things you can do if someone else begins and how to successfully continue from there

1) React

This is what you've probably been doing your whole life when someone starts anything with you anyway, but let's label it, so we are now more aware we are doing it. Someone does a thing to initiate, and you simply react to it.

> PERSON 1: *This cheese dip is so good, don't you think?*
> PERSON 2: *Oh wow, I was actually afraid to try it and was waiting for someone to get in there first. But if you say it's good, then let's go!*

This is best done with an emotional reaction instead of a neutral one. But if you do react neutrally with no defined emotion- you can guess what I'm going to say next: get that emotion as soon as you can. It always goes back to having that emotion to respond from.

2) Match

With this method, we simply Match (or Mirror) the initiation the other person just did. Did they sigh? You sigh too. Did they start to test an invisible microphone? You do that thing as well! Did they start with a clear emotion? Oh yes, you better match the heck out of that!

> PERSON 1: *This cheese dip is so good, don't you think?*
> PERSON 2: *Right? It's so good I can't stop eating it!*

We've talked endlessly about having an emotion at the start of an improv scene and real-life interaction. Some of you may have held on to the idea that you can pre-plan an emotion and feel safe doing that- at least improv doesn't mean that everyone is coming up with things in the moment, and I can still think ahead!

Well, here is a great example of why any sort of pre-planning, even thinking of your emotion, can get in your way. If someone initiates and you match them, that will probably conflict with the emotion you thought of. So instead of that last remaining pre-planning safety net of having your emotion thought up beforehand, let the other person just give it to you by you having nothing in mind and only grabbing that emotion as soon as you match another person.

This might be difficult at first because it may be too frightening to have really nothing at all in your head when going into an improv scenario. But that's the goal of everything we've been talking about- get out of your head, and listen in the moment. Everything is right here in front of us, and if we pay attention to the now, we don't have to worry about what to do- just listen and respond.

Most of us as humans (sorry for any robots reading this) like to be around and interact with people who are similar to us. Think about it, aren't most of your friends your friends because you have very specific things in common? Maybe hobbies, or outlook on the world, or music- people like to be around those who match us. It probably goes back to a pre-historic human element of being safe and accepted by our family tribe- going out on your own and finding a different tribe could mean your demise. Things aren't really like this anymore, but we still hold that instinct to enjoy being around those people who are similar to us.

Plus, matching is a great way to connect that other person and us immediately in that moment. We are both clearly listening to each other and building this interaction together when we match; everyone wants to be heard and listened to.

3) Opposite

This is the reverse of Matching. If the other person initiates with a sign, we do the opposite. Maybe we reply with a big smile on our faces.[31] We just have to take a different point of view or emotion than how the other person began.

In improv scenes, this works great because since both characters are in the same environment dealing with the same thing, we get to see how two people can feel very differently about the same thing which usually leads to funny situations. But does replying in an opposite manner also work in real life? Yep. Now let's take our cheese dip example again:

> PERSON 1: *This cheese dip is so good, don't you think?*
> PERSON 2: *No, it's the most disgusting thing I've ever had in my life.*

Since we said how humans like to be around other humans the same as us, responding like this will probably distance you from having a good

---

[31] Is that the opposite of a sigh? I don't know, it's whatever you think it is. There's no wrong answer remember!

interaction or connection with the other person. You could still do it, if you aren't looking for those things, but I think that's not why you bought a book on how to use improv in life. You probably want to increase your chances of having better interactions, not terrible ones. But...you can still use opposite reacting as a method...by *joking* that you feel that way.

> PERSON 1: *This cheese dip is so good, don't you think?*
> PERSON 2: *No, it's the most disgusting thing I've ever had in my life. I probably will never eat another bite of any food because it ruined everything for me!*

Reading that as Person 2 is serious is someone you'd walk away from. But reading it as someone who is saying that very *sarcastically* (hey now, that's emotion!) will give you a fun place to start in the interaction. It shows that you don't take things so seriously and like joking around and having fun.

In that chapter, we'll talk more about comedy, but to add a bit more here, it's all about being clear that you aren't serious. Maybe it's a voice you put on, or grand gestures- anything that a real person wouldn't really do in this situation. You aren't a jerk; you're pretending to say what a jerk might say in this situation, and letting the other person know it's all pretend with a smile on your face, and a giggle on your lips.

Now I realize that doing the Opposite or Matching in themselves are Reactions. But again, we're breaking these methods down, so you have clear options in your brain. Previously, when someone started talking to us, we probably didn't think of how we would respond and just started talking - no self awareness and thus no idea how to continue from there, and definitely wouldn't have had the option in our mind that you could respond my Matching. But now you do.

Honor The Initiation

A few paragraphs ago, we talked about not "being that person" – the person who steamrolls and only pushes their own ideas in an interaction. We've all seen that person, and they are exhausting to have conversations with. In improv, it's even worse because that person breaks all the improv rules to be the funniest one on stage there, but really it's all very confusing for the audience and the performers.

The way to make sure this is never you is to [insert improv rule here...listen; Yes, And; be present, etc]. If someone else starts before you, then whatever idea or initiation you had in mind that was ready to be used, throw it away and focus on what's happening right now instead. As soon as someone approaches your awareness to start talking to you, they get to initiate- that's why they approached you. Maybe they don't have anything substantial, but they moved first. So it's your responsibility to honor their move, give them your attention, and react to them. In a way, you could look at this as *Yessing* them, but not adding that *And*...just yet. If, after a few moments, you can see they have nothing but bravely started first anyway, then you can do something else to get the conversation moving. For example:

> PERSON 1: *Oh hey!*
> PERSON 2: (matching) *Hey!*
> PERSON 1: *How's it going?*
> PERSON 2: *Good, and you?*
> PERSON 1: *Good.*

Okay, by now, we can tell that even though they started, they don't have much else, so we can add other stuff to help the conversation move. What stuff? Well, we should already have our emotion since it's been a few sentences, and from that we can use any of those six ways to initiate to go further: Emotion, Posture, Word, Sound, Physical Action, parts of CREW.

To further hit home the idea of honoring the person who started, I once did an improv scene where me and my scene partner stepped on stage *almost* at the same time, and since neither of us knew who was technically first, we both waited for the other person to start the scene- but no one did. So we stood there staring at each other, doing absolutely nothing else until one of our teammates had the perfect instinct to end the scene.

You may be thinking, "Well, that's a dumb scene. It had nothing to it. Why would you include that example?" But wait, you didn't let me finish (rude!). After a few other scenes, myself and that same person found ourselves both onstage again, and we noticed that, so we both did the exact same thing again, nothing! The "scene" ended and seemed pointless yet again.

After that, we did this a third time, which suddenly got huge applause from the audience for the callback and comedy 'rule of three' even though nothing else happened in the scene.[32]

There was no CREW at all and while this may have looked like a terrible improv scene, what we did was follow the main improv rules! We *listened* to each other, noticing the situation we found ourselves in. We *agreed* to continue with what we had done, which in itself was matching each other's *initiation* of doing nothing. And we supported each other by not breaking the thing we started with by trying to suddenly make a scene of it. The scene was, in reality, the lack of doing a scene. So in a way, we did have CREW. We were playing improvisers on a team, doing an improv scene in this theater. Meta, but it worked! All the rules of improv can be broken only if all members of the team agree to break them, which we did here by not saying or doing anything else.

Like many of the techniques we are talking about in this here book, it all comes down to that first rule, Listening. Be present and use that present

---

[32] See chapter on Comedy for what those things even are!

moment to create what we're going to do next, even if it's just building off someone else who started.

EXERCISE: Mirror

We think about ourselves all day long, but this exercise shifts the focus onto the other person. Using your improv skills, see how long you can have a great conversation with someone by matching them. You'll be surprised how much people open up and talk with someone similar to themselves. This can't be planned, but it's an exercise you can put into action when the moment presents itself.

IMPROV EXERCISE

MIRROR

Skills Used:
Self-Awareness + Connecting to others

1 Next time you are talking to someone, start to mirror and match them.

2 Stand in the same posture as them (i.e. arms crossed, eye contact, slouching or not, etc)

3 Also mirror their speech (i.e. repeat some words they say or the emotion in which they speak from)

4 Do these without mocking them or them even noticing you are doing it.

5 Once you've done this for a while, see if you can change your posture and if they will subconsciously mirror you!

The **goal** of this exercise is to show you that you never need to worry about what to say because most people will say everything for you. We don't like silence, and if we are in the company of someone similar to us, people are very open to having conversation with others who "get them."

Now I'm not suggesting any manipulation at all here- don't use these skills to get information or talk to someone in the hope of using it against them in some way. This is all for your journey along becoming for creativity and showcasing your personality, while getting the fear and mental blocks out of the way. As we said, as soon as we interact with someone else, we are in a relationship with them. Even if it's only a relationship that last two minutes, respect that relationship as if it were to last years.

CHAPTER 8
THE SUGGESTION

If you've ever been to an improv show, then you are probably familiar with what the *Suggestion* from the audience, also known as the *Ask For* is. It's the one time that the crowd can talk to the performers while they are onstage and have a direct influence on the show. But what's the point? Why do improvisers even need the audience to give them an idea for the show? Shouldn't they be creative enough to come up with ideas for the show you paid to watch?

Well, there's a major purpose of the Suggestion and that's to prove to the audience that what they are doing on stage is indeed improv. If a group came out and just started performing, who's to say they didn't write the show and rehearse it with memorized lines the night before? But having a random audience member shout something out, and they do an entire improv performance based on that proves that they are making it up. And no, I've never heard of a group having a plant in the audience yell out a specific thing so that the group can do their written material and have a better show. Improv people love improvising and take every opportunity to do what they love in front of anyone who will watch.

There's another purpose of the suggestion, though, to give you the improviser a jumping-off point. If you really were to do an improvised show without a suggestion, without a 'topic' of suggestion, you could do infinite things, and we said before, having to decide what to do with infinite options would stop your brain from deciding on anything. But, by getting the audience to *suggest* something, allows them to have a focus, that of which is whatever it is they suggested to you for the show.

So how does this help us, in life? Usually, we don't go through the day, and someone shouts a word out at us, "Pancakes!" and expect us to do a 25-minute performance off of that. But, we still can use the concept of the improv suggestion as a jumping off point for our daily, unexpected, situations we end up in.

As we talked about in our chapter on Initiations, we can do anything to start, but that also means being *inspired by* anything. Everything around us can inspire what to say and do next, if only we can get out of our heads and be present enough to notice it. That first rule of improv, Listening, will help us out here.

Listen and be aware of what is happening around you, using all your senses- what you hear, see, feel, smell, and taste- to inspire you. Thinking like this, it seems ridiculous to think that we aren't sure what to say in any situation. That's not really the issue. The issue is that we're too up in our heads looking for the answer when it's right out in front of us.

To this end, let's say you are in an improv scenario somewhere with someone- I'll leave it up to you to fill in the blanks for this imaginary example, and you aren't sure what to say next (either in starting or reaching a silent dead end in the middle of talking with this someone). In order not to just stare blankly at the other person waiting for them to save the chat, you notice an indoor plant in the corner of the room. For this example, "indoor plant" will be our suggestion and here are some ways to let it inspire you:

Use Initiation Techniques

Without copying and pasting the entire previous chapter here in what would be an endless loop, you can use any of the approaches discussed there connecting to our suggestion of "indoor plant." Need me to go further? Flip back a few pages and try some out yourself, I can't do all the work for ya!

Third Thought vs. A-to-C

This improv concept of *Third Thought* and *A-to-C* are the exact same thing with two different names. "Third Thought" was an idea coined by Del Close[33] , which means don't go directly with what the subject is, but look into the larger possible meaning of the thing. At UCB[34] this same concept is called "A to C" in which we aren't supposed to use the *A* (first) idea. Think a little deeper and use our *C* (third) idea. For example, if the suggestion was "coffee," don't just talk about drinking coffee, but think into further ideas such as drug runners in Columbia or someone with an addiction- all of which were inspired by the idea of 'coffee.'

Using our "indoor plant" suggestions, some *Third Thought/A-to-C* examples could be:

- do plants get jealous looking out the window at outdoor plants?
- or do they brag they don't have to deal with nature's elements anymore?
- to survive, indoor plants need sunshine, water, and soil, but do they also require the smell of human food cooking in the next room and TV show background noise?

---

[33] Del Close is known as the father of modern improvisation. I probably mentioned him somewhere else in this book, and might do it again. But if not, that's who he is and improv probably wouldn't be well-known at all without him.

[34] An improv theater that was created by former students of Del Close: Amy Poehler, Matt Walsh, Ian Roberts, and Matt Besser being the core founders.

- do they ever get sick on getting fed splashes of tap water and would much rather have a glass of wine like the humans do?
- do we own the plants, or are they really in charge, as if we don't take care of their every need, they start to wilt?

...SO we could use any of these, and definitely more, to start an interesting topic of discussion. The topics don't have to be real, actual things we believe (like plants needing TV sounds), but could be an amusing thing to discuss anyway, for the fun of it. Using *Third Thought/A-to-C* techniques will get you to more creative, original ideas instead of just talking about, "I wonder how much water they give that indoor plant," and will set you apart as someone more creative and fun to be around.

Use Your Memories

As we went over way back in one of the first chapters, anyone can be good at improv because we have memories to pull from, and this is a great moment to put those to use.

Simply think of a memory you have related to the suggestion and use that as a jumping off point of conversation. For example, when I think of the word "indoor plant," I think of how I attempted to have my own house plants a few years ago, ones that "survive well without direct sunshine and are hard to kill" yet, sure enough, they didn't prevail in my house, and I must just be doomed to ever have a living plant.

Now we have a new topic of discussion that can be expanded upon using the many ways we've already talked about. To be clear, the exchange between you and the other person might not only be about you and your story, because that would be forcing your own ideas, but it gives you a jumping off point that both of you can work with. If the topic of discussion goes to something else, stay in the moment and build off of that, all of which was directly, or indirectly inspired by a true memory you had.

Another way we could do this is by using what the suggestion means to you. If you love plants, use that emotion and go! Or do the opposite and start by saying "I can't stand indoor plants! They need to be set free!" Again, the opposite usually lends itself to a more made-up scenario and not how you really feel, but could all be in jest.[35]

The point is that the suggestion can be used in multiple ways outside of talking about something on a surface level, "oh wow, plants are green, and need water..." Make it personal and specific by using any of the above.

Summary of Ways to Use the Suggestion:

- Ways to initiate (Word, Sound, Physical Action, Emotion, Posture, CREW)
- Think of other ideas related to the suggestion (Third Thought/A-to-C)
- Use your own memories or feeling towards that suggestion.

---

[35] I would never say the word "jest" in real life, but it fit so well in that sentence, how could I not.

EXERCISE: Advanced Thinking

This exercise will work on the concepts of Third-Thought thinking and help you access ideas further in your brain instead of only surface-levels ideas.

ADVANCED THINKING

Skills Used:
* Third Thoughts
* Creativity
* Quicker Thinking

How to Do It:

1 Either out loud or written down start with a random word.

2 This is similar to Word Association, but instead, the first word you think of will be said to yourself/not written down.

3 As quickly as you can say/write the next word you think of.

4 Then do the same thing, skipping the next word, but saying or writing down the following word, trying to get to that word faster each time.

Goal:
To be able to access those further ideas (aka Third Thought or A-C ideas) quicker, instead of stopping your ind only at the first thing that you come up with.

There Are No Bad Suggestions

That's right. There are no bad suggestions, only less-creative ways of using them. Since our goal is to find new and creative topics and ideas from a random word we get from our surroundings or what someone said, it shouldn't matter what that word is. Everything can lead to heaps of new ideas unless we're taking it a boring face value. Just like our example of "indoor plant" from above...yes, talking about indoor plants sounds pretty mundane and could be looked at as a bad suggestion, but only if we are taking about them at the surface level and not using these methods to go further with the suggestion.

But what if it really is a "bad" suggestion? What if someone says the word 'poop" or "spatula?"[36] Great, then use that suggestion just as you normally would, instead of trying to look for the better thing as a jumping off point. Again, there are no bad suggestions, only lackluster ways to use it.

Look, no one really wants to have a long conversation about spatulas (except maybe a kitchen tool aficionado), but if the topic comes up, either as a random thing someone just happened to say or as a challenge to try and stump you, take it anyway, and amaze them that you can make something interesting about whatever is thrown your way.

I Don't Know That Suggestion, Though!

What if you get a suggestion and don't know what the person just said? I'm telling you to go with the first thing you hear, but even in this instance? Yes. Why? BECAUSE THERE'S NO WRONG ANSWER BUT NO ANSWER.

---

[36] Spatula is the most common improv suggestion. True story.

Let's say someone said, "Paul Butterfield." If you don't know whom I'm referencing, then you would just go with whom you think that is:

- Is it a guy who owns a Butter farm?[37]
- Is he Mrs. Butterworth's neighbor?
- Maybe it's some baseball player from the 80s.

The point is it doesn't matter as long as you create from it. In fact, not knowing something but going with it anyway is a win-win situation. And here's why.

If there are people in attendance who also don't know who or what that suggestion is, they'll assume that you do since you so confidently went along with it and added other information (Yes, And) and think how smart and knowledgeable you are. Great job!

On the other hand, for those who know Paul Butterfield, I'm referring to the Chicago blues who had big hits in the 1960s, and you run with talking about a butter farmer, they will think you are being funny and laugh at your comedic ability and originality. If, and when, someone corrects you and says, "That's not who I meant." you would still say Yes, And even that statement, "I know, that was a different Butterfield." Another great job!

So it's a win-win, and the only way you lose-lose is if we stand there and hem and haw and act like we don't know what to do with that suggestion we were given. Guess what? It's improv...no one knows what they are doing. That's the point. But the purpose of it is to make something up, so get to the making up something!

---

[37] Wait, is there such a thing as a butter farm, or is this just known as a dairy farm?

No Suggestions

Before we close this chapter, I want to talk about not having a suggestion. As said, the improv suggestion gives us something to go off. However, I would be remiss if I didn't mention one of the best improv shows we can see, TJ and Dave[38] who simply begin their shows by saying, "Trust us, this is all made up" and when the lights go down and back up, they just look at each other and start there races for one of the smartest, well played two-person shows you will see.

But there is no suggestion from the audience, so it's really pre-planned, right? Nope! When the lights go down, both people choose a posture (ding, ding- one of the ways to initiate), and when the lights come up, they each *react* to what they see the other person doing. So, in reality, they are still reacting to something, it just so happens to be a random pose each of them takes once on stage, which acts as their suggestion. So even with no blatant suggestion, they are still inspired by what's around them.

There we have it. Suggestions. Now I *suggest* we move on to the next chapter.[39]

---

[38] TJ Jagodowski and Dave Pasquesi in Chicago. They have a book too. Check it out!

[39] This is a dumb joke, but I left it in the book anyway because it was just dumb enough.

EXERCISE: Suggestion List

Skills Used:

* Quick-Thinking
* Being inspired by the Suggestion

To put all the techniques learned in this chapter to use, you can do this exercise any time without needing anyone else, or even paper and writing utensils. Yes, saving trees!

IMPROV EXERCISE

SUGGESTION LIST

How to Do It:

01 Get a random suggestion *(from a book, social media, and a random song lyric, etc.)*

02 Talk/Write out all the different ways you can use that suggestion to inspire new ideas and thoughts using the methods listed in the chapter.

03 Repeat with a new subject

Talking about ideas when you're in a no-pressure place (like at home, or in the car) will allow your brain to make the connections without the tension of people watching you. The **goal** is to show you that no matter what you get, you can find an interesting way to use it. Plus, once you come up with one idea, that can become a new suggestion and inspire even more, linked from that first word.

EXERCISE: Object Monologue

I first came across this exercise from legendary improv teacher and director Mick Napier.[40] It's a bit like the fun kids' game Madlibs. I know, I know, I said some of these warm-ups are like kid's games, but this one really is similar!

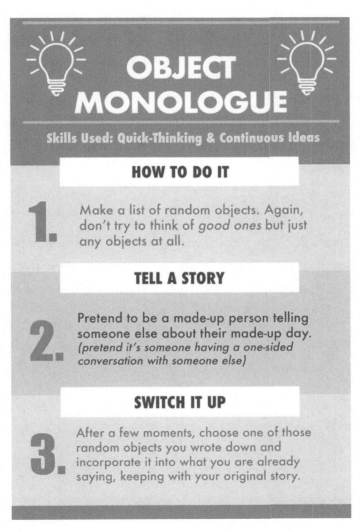

OBJECT MONOLOGUE

Skills Used: Quick-Thinking & Continuous Ideas

HOW TO DO IT

1. Make a list of random objects. Again, don't try to think of *good ones* but just any objects at all.

TELL A STORY

2. Pretend to be a made-up person telling someone else about their made-up day. *(pretend it's someone having a one-sided conversation with someone else)*

SWITCH IT UP

3. After a few moments, choose one of those random objects you wrote down and incorporate it into what you are already saying, keeping with your original story.

---

[40] Check out his book for other great improv exercises and wisdom.
Mick Napier, *Improvise: Scene from the Inside Out* (Meriwether Publishing Ltd; 2015)

Object Monologue Example:

PERSON ONE: *Well, let me tell you, I had quite the week. On my way to work yesterday I got a flat tire and had to pull over on the highway to fix it. Good thing I had a* (Seeing the word "Tea Kettle" on list) *Tea Kettle in my backseat, though! I was able to throw it at a passing car and have them pull over and help me fix the tire. But first they really wanted to talk about* (Seeing the word "Pencil" on the list) *Pencils. So there we stood for three hours talking about writing tools.*

The **goal** is to think on your feet and integrate new ideas while simultaneously staying focused and being able to continue your story. Improv is a lot like spinning plates or juggling; you have to be able to do multiple things at once.

Tips:

- Again, don't try to pick the right word. Just randomly point to one and force yourself to use it in your story, even if you think it doesn't make sense. Justification is all part of improvised creativity.

CHAPTER 9
HOW TO BE FUNNY

The task of sitting down to write only one chapter on comedy is a big undertaking, and luckily I'm not the first person to write on the subject. There are a plethora of books and resources to learn about comedy these days. Humor is something that it has existed since the dawn of human civilization, and as such, people have been telling other people how to do it ever since. We like to laugh at things because it releases tension from everyday life's hardships and stress. Just as crying, shouting, or sighing, are all releases of emotion During certain instances in our life, so is laughter in comedy.

As we said before, you may have picked up this book because you saw the word improv and wanted to learn how to be funnier also, as we said before, while improv doesn't have to equal comedy, most people associate the two together, well because making stuff up on the spot is usually funny. So we put it off long enough. How about we learn to be a little bit more humorous in our lives? The following are some specific techniques of Comedy that can use to be funnier. It's not an exhaustive list or the be and end-all how to be funny, but they're just some techniques that you may find helpful.

Be Creative:

If you are not prioritizing being more creative in your everyday life, then you are really missing the whole point of reading this book. The dictionary defines Creativity as "making or bringing into existence something new."

Well, that's a pretty powerful skill if I do say so myself. But sadly, I've worked with many clients and companies who are "too busy" to ever think about being creative in their lives. And as such, nothing is very exciting to them. Even now, ask yourself what excites you and you're looking forward to. If you can't think of anything, it's a good time to start being more creative in your life, and comedians are some of the most creative people[41].

Good comedians don't take anything for granted. We ask why and we're curious about the world, looking at it from a perspective as if it's a new thing we've never seen before. We metaphorically take apart the entire car and put it back together in a way that probably doesn't work as efficiently, but is much more interesting. When we see something, even a common everyday routine, location, or task, we break it down to the root element of it and look at it from a different perspective. We ask ourselves what's interesting, strange, or unique or weird about this subject? This is where new ideas come in the world, from always being curious and wondering about things.

To be more creative, don't take things at face value. Yes, there are plenty of things that we see in our life every day that we don't even think about doing - using the bathroom, watching our teeth, cooking food, driving to work, ordering a drink at the bar, doing laundry, laying down to sleep at night- we all know what that looks like. But if you look at those tasks as if you are an alien from another planet who just landed on Earth and really have no understanding of them, you can look at them from a new point of view and find what's interesting about them. Isn't it interesting that all humans lay horizontal to sleep? What if, instead, we had to lean against a wall to sleep? Well, now there's a brand new concept. Or instead of putting

---

[41] Good good comedians anyway, I'm not talking about the kind to her always and complain about everything and don't actually have any humor and anything they do. Those kind of comedians are playing the role of "look at me I'm a comedian, so I complain about everything" which is based off of an old style of comedy from the 90s. But true comedians are creative who look for fun in everything

toothpaste on a toothbrush to brush your teeth and putting laundry washing machine to wash clothes, they were swapped. Now we put detergent in our mouth, swish it around, and toothpaste on each item of clothing to get them washed. Another creative, different idea.

To be more creative just start looking at things a different way. This is your first step to strengthening your sense of humor and being more skilled at being funny.

Think about one of the funniest things you have seen on TV or in a movie. Chances are high it was funny to you because it was something that demonstrated something from a different point of view. It may have been something you relate to under extremely unique circumstances. That all starts from just being a little bit more creative, and like all of the skills mentioned in this book, strengthening your creativity and comedy quickness takes time and practice to improve. But you'll never get better if you don't start now.

Playing Pretend

One of the easiest ways to sharpen your wit skills is to play pretend more often. Now after reading what I just wrote you might be thinking 'why did I buy this book to help with my adult life when we're going to talk about playing pretend? I'm not a child! I'm a grown up!" Well, if you think that, then it's exactly why you're probably reading this book.

The Improv Mindset is always looking for the fun in everything, including playing a bit of pretend. For some reason our society has taught us that once you grow up, you're not allowed to have an imagination anymore, as if a creative mind is something bad. Yet what do all adults do in their free time? Watch hours and hours of movies and TV on screens that all tell imaginative stories. Isn't that interesting? So I don't care how old you are, or how mature you think you are, it's time to start awakening the inner child again and playing pretend.

All right now by pretend I don't necessarily mean sitting on the floor playing with plastic toys made for kids - but you're more than welcome to if you want. I'm talking about having a little bit more fun in your day-to-day and adding a little bit of pretend to some of life's random moments. This is all about practicing your improv skills, and many of the examples in the Improv Scenario chapter are all about playing pretend too.

A simple way to do this is just to change your emotion. Maybe instead of acting neutral or a little friendly the next time you order a coffee at your local nationwide chain coffeehouse, why not act like you are the most excited person in the world to get this cup of overpriced joe? Or pretend that getting the coffee is the climax of an action adventure movie, and you finally found the lost treasure and now you get to celebrate it- by adding non-dairy creamer and sugar. Or when you're grocery shopping, in your mind, choose one person in the store that is your archenemy, and you have to make it through all of the aisles without crossing paths with them.

These are little games that kids would play, but then their adult handlers tell them to stop goofing off and take things seriously. Well, I'm giving you permission to start goofing off and take things not as seriously!

You can do these on your own, but they're a lot more fun to do with a group of friends. This brings us to the idea, technique, and incredible art of comedy bits.

Bits, also known as a wonderful side effect of people who start to learn Improv, are a great way to practice your skills of improv all day, every day with anyone or even anything you interact with.

The easiest way to describe bits is to think about the greatest memory you have of hanging out with your best friends and laughing so hard that your sides hurt. When you think back on the hangout in the morning, it's still the funniest thing you've ever heard. Then you try to explain it to someone who wasn't here, and suddenly it's not as funny, and something get's lost in the telling of the Bit. You had to be there.

Comedy bits are exactly that- small pieces of jokes and humor about anything at all. This could be pretending a can of soup can talk or that every time you say a certain word you say it in a weird voice, make a pun about something, or make up a fake answer to a question someone asks you. Bits are anything that you have fun with and make a joke about. These aren't full improv scenes where there's a story, or even an emotion, but they're funny bite-sized pieces of comedy that you can do anywhere. Basically, if you've ever made a joke or were "playing around" with someone before and they asked you if you were serious and you said 'I'm just kidding'... that's a bit!

Just like joking around with your best friends is more fun than joking around by yourself, practicing bits with friends is a blast. In fact, you probably have been doing this for years and didn't even realize it. It's really just playing pretend for short moments of time. They exist in scripted comedy too. Any scene that has something funny happen but isn't the main focus of the scene is a bit! See you know all about bits and playing pretend, and there you thought pretending was just for children.

But a warning before going crazy with your bits- don't lie to people. I feel like the difference between a bit or a joke, and a lie is if you leave that person thinking that what you said was true, that's a lie. But if, before you leave them for the day, you let them in on the joke, it's not a lie. So when you practice your bittiness, make sure you let other people know that you're doing a bit, so they don't just think you're a pathological liar. An easy way to let them know you are joking is to say and do your bits with a smile. I learned this the hard way, as I'm a sucker for dry humor. I would do bits completely straight aced, and no one would ever know when I was joking or not, which usually meant they couldn't join along either. But if you say your bit as *if you are doing a bit*, then everyone gets to join along, and they'll see you as someone who likes to have fun. This is usually for people who don't know you that well. With your friends, you can do this all day and they'll probably join in... and you don't have to explain yourself. That's why bits with friends are the most fun.

So practice bits in every circumstance that you can (appropriately) and notice how it strengthens your improv muscles at the same time. Also, a handy side effect of 'doing bits' is that it makes you not take everything so seriously and have a little bit more fun in life. And we can all do with more of that.

Rule of Three & Rule of Infinite

Another device of drollery we've actually already discussed which is the Callback. Again, in comedy, this is an idea or subject that was already mentioned that is 'called-back' into the present moment (be it a long form improvisation performance or a conversation). It's funny because everyone gets the reference to something that was already said, but seemed to forget about. But not you, because you Listen and pay attention and are reading a book on improv!

We also talked about how if you attempt a callback joke and it lands flat (doesn't work, doesn't get a laugh, etc.), you can try it again until it works. This brings us to what's known as the Comedy Rules of Three.

Humans are natural pattern appreciators - we love getting into a routine, no matter how weird. Like someone who 'always drinks their coffee with their non-dominant hand.' Sure it's messy, but to them, it's good luck.[42] When we do or see something occur just once, it's random to us. But then, if it happens multiple times, it becomes normal, and even humorous, especially when it happens three times.

For example, let's say you are sitting at an outdoor café doing some people watching (a great way to inspire your Improv Mindset, by the way), and you notice a spot on the sidewalk that someone trips on a little. They don't fall down, and it's barely noticeable, but they catch their foot just right on some uneven pavement.

The first time you see this, you probably think, 'oh, wow, glad that person didn't fall.' But then it happens to someone else. Now you think, 'what's with that spot? Someone should fix that.' And then it happens to a third person. This time you probably let out a little chuckle and think, 'There's that silly sidewalk again.' That is the comedy Rule of Three.

The rule officially states something, anything, happening once is odd, a second time interesting, but a third time it's funny. Three dots make a pattern and a natural pattern was created by something happening a third time. It's also funny to us because we prefer things in even numbers (six pack of beer, four pack of hotdogs, 18 wheeler truck...okay that may be for safety's sake, but you get the point). But something being an odd number registers in our brain as odd, different, and funny.

Here's another example from my own life. A friend of mine had a very sarcastic sounding laugh, even when he was laughing for real, in all honesty. Whenever he would be at a live comedy show and would naturally laugh, people in the audience would look at him, thinking he was being rude. When he would laugh a second time, fewer people looked, and everyone

---

[42] We all know someone who does this, right? No? That's maybe because I just made up a random weird routine.

else just found it normal – there's that sarcastic guy again. But the third time he laughed, the audience laughed along with him! This made for any show he was attending extra funny because there would be double laughter-first from something that happened on stage, and then another round of laughs in reaction to my friend's unique way of chuckling.

So that's how the Comedy Rule of Three works which brings us to the Comedy Rule of Infinite. Like the previous rule, this idea states that the more something happens it will eventually become funny again. It's really a continuation of the Rule of Three. Let's break it down.

When something first happens, it's odd. The second time it's interesting. The third time it's funny. But then the fourth time, it's odd again. Why is that still happening? The same goes for the fifth, sixth, seventh, and so on. At this point, we sort of forget about it even going on. It's become expected and normal to us. But eventually, at one point, it will come back around and become funny again, which is usually even funnier than the third time it happened! That's the Rule of Infinite.

Going back to our uneven sidewalk example, after the fourth, fifth, sixth, etc. person trips, you just become used to that damn tricky sidewalk. Well, back to enjoying your gluten-free crumble cake and foamy latte (we're at an outdoor café, remember?). But suddenly, the 12th person trips on the sidewalk, and you chuckle again. Then as it keeps happening with different people, you feel the urge to point it out to the person next to you (or film it on your phone because that's more of what happens these days. It's so funny to you that you want to let other people in on the joke. And that's all thanks to the Rule of Infinite- and poor cement construction.

That's why if you bring a Callback into a conversation and it doesn't work, keep trying. If it still doesn't get a laugh on the third try, then go full force forward and keep trying because chances are very likely that it will eventually get a laugh, all thanks because you know this powerful comedy technique.

The Secret to Comedy

So we learned to do bits and use callbacks several times. But what do you choose to do those things about, and what do we say to be funnier in life? Well, that's where the secret to comedy comes in....shhh, don't tell anyone!

Before we go on, remember that improv doesn't have to be funny. It just has to be improvised. However, since most people want to learn improv to become funnier, I will let you in on this little secret, a secret to what makes us laugh.

To me, the secret of comedy is Opposites. By opposites, I mean something unexpected and outside of the normal way of thinking. Take a look at this example:

> Normal: A Doctor gives test results to a patient in their office. *(not funny)*
> Opposite: A doctor gives test results to a patient at the patient's home while the patient is showering. *(funnier!)*
> Normal: The test results say the patient has one week to live. *(not funny)*
> Opposite: The test results say that the patient is invincible and will live forever. *(funnier!)*
> Normal: the doctor is a human. *(not funny)*
> Opposite: The doctor is a talking dolphin, and they are at Sea World. *(funnier!)*

See, each of the opposites has more chances are being funny. I'm not saying the normal examples aren't good enough. They completely are. But if you want to add more humor to your improv scenarios, use opposites.

Now by Opposites, I don't mean random and crazy. If your opposite is too out there, it will just be confusing. If the doctor had a lizard tail but was also a dolphin, and they were flying a spaceship that runs off of almond butter fuel, and they're listening to a Danish cover band of The Beatles.... that's not funny, and I'm just lost on what we were even talking about.

A good way to think of Opposites is to keep it specific and something different than the obvious for a piece of CREW (Character, Relationship, Environment, and Why...as a refresher). A doctor in an office is normal, but a doctor visiting you at home while you are showering is less obvious, thus, funnier. A doctor who is actually a dolphin is even less expected, so even more humorous. The more surprising the choice is, the funnier it will be because it's unexpected.

Again think of the funniest shows, movies, or jokes you heard. They were funny because they weren't in line with normal everyday life. The character of Kramer on *Seinfeld* is funny because he doesn't act like a real person. He doesn't work, he has crazy hair, and he walks into a room differently than anybody should. So we laugh. This is why the method of joke writing with a Setup and Punchline also works.

A well-written joke starts with a Setup- which creates a set world or idea in our head (something normal we can all get on board with or recognize), and then the Punchline simply twists that setup into a different circumstance (something unexpected and opposite). Here's a setup & punchline joke example I found online:

> Setup: My boss accused me of being immature.
> Punchline: I told them to get out of my pillow fort.

The setup creates a world in which you assume the person is not immature but an everyday boring person, maybe even one you associate with someone you picture in your head. Then the punchline is surprising, or the opposite, because they admit to being immature and still build forts.[43]

Now while using improv, I'm not saying we're going to go into conversations trying to make two-liner jokes, or any pre-planned jokes for that matter, but I used this as an easy example to demonstrate Opposite, and also teach Setup and Punchline since it's a tried and true comedy method. Again, think about the least expected place, response, or relationship to a situation, and you'll probably find some comedy. A situation between two friends arguing about who ate the last slice of pizza would be very different if those two people were pretending to be the Monarch of the UK and their significant other. Opposites!

---

[43] I implore you to build a pillow fort as an adult. It's so much fun and no one will tell you to clean up your mess!

EXERCISE: Comedy Opposites

Let's start thinking more comedically using this exercise. Comedy all comes from surprising opposites!

IMPROV EXERCISE OPPOSITES

Skills Used:
Comedic Ability, Imagination, Creativity

1 Write down a random noun *(person, place, or object)*

2 Below it, write down opposite ideas related it

3 Ideas such as where it wouldn't be, who wouldn't be there, what you wouldn't use it for, etc.

4 The more you can write down, the stronger your sense of humor is growing.

5 Repeat the process with a different noun and make your brain funnier!

Loosen Up

Here's an additional technique we can use to be more comical in our life. Simply loosen up a little. Instead of trying so hard to be funny, or on the other end, taking everything so seriously and making a drama out of every situation- take it easy.

First of all, many of these techniques will come naturally to us just by simply cooling down some. Practicing them will definitely help, but if we're uptight about everything, it's going to be a lot harder to get creative and strengthen our sense of comedic ability. Look, sometimes things don't go our way, and this is really what we've been talking about throughout this book and what it means to be in that Improv Mindset.

With improv, we can't force our own ideas, and we have to be open to the possibility of things going unexpectedly and being able to think on our toes and roll with all the erratic punches. So when things in life don't go as planned, or a person doesn't act the way we want them to, we have to let it go and stay present. The more we hold on to drama and repeat all the stories of all the bad things that happened to us, the more of those events will happen in our life because we're focusing on it.

Instead, we can breathe and use the techniques we talked about already to be present in the moment, which will open us up to new circumstances that have the opportunity to be better for us.

Also, no one likes being around someone who's filled with drama and who takes everything so seriously. Life itself is confusing and sometimes very difficult, and everyone is dealing with something in their own life. So to be someone that only communicates through the emotion of frustration, anger, or spite is going to be someone that nobody really wants to be around in the first place. And if no one wants to be around you, then there's no way you can practice any of these techniques talked about in this book. So chill out!

In my own life, I've come to learn that the more I take things with a grain of salt and look for humor in everything, the easier life becomes. I try to have a life attitude like that of water. Water can flow around any object. Water can fit into any shape. Water can change temperatures very easily, and water doesn't get mad when your friend cancels on you ten minutes before they're supposed to meet you for lunch. Things happen, but if I keep the mindset of being present and be that of water, things can flow past me without ruining my day.

Of course, I'm not saying you should be a pushover and not stand up for yourself or your personal boundaries. Absolutely you should. Being relaxed and looking for fun in every situation doesn't mean you should lose your personal power. Everyone is different and has different expectations for situations, but if you feel like your boundaries are being pushed, or you're being disrespected and you need to stand up for yourself, go ahead and do it. But one of the most powerful things is to be unaffected by all the effects of the world. This is what improv teaches us. Be present, listen, and react to what's right in front of you, consciously choosing your own emotion instead of a knee jerk reaction based on a past version of yourself (you know, before you started learning how to use improv).

This takes a lot of practice, but the more we are present in the now, the less we will be affected by the simple hardships of life. And this will open us up to being more creative and funnier people than we used to be.

Comedy is Subjective

It's true that comedy really is subjective. No matter how much we learn to do it and study the art of being funny, something that is hilarious to one person just isn't funny to another. A lot of what we find funny is based on our upbringing and the current lifestyle that we are in. If the funniest show on TV were all about football, I probably wouldn't enjoy it as someone who's not a big fan of the pigskin.

But being subjective shouldn't be an excuse for not being funny. I've seen a lot of comedians come, and always go, who would blame the audience for why they didn't get any laughs. Thinking that their comedy was too *blank* (cerebral, silly, advanced or unique), they would say the reason that their show didn't go well was because the audience "didn't get it." But that's not an excuse to be bad at comedy.

Wherever we're trying to be funny, whether on stage or making jokes in a conversation, we have to read the room and know our audience. If we're communicating with a bunch of middle-aged dads and we're making jokes about social media, of course, they're not going to laugh because they don't get what we're talking about. We have the ability to dodge comedy subjectivity by simply recognizing who is the receiver of our jokes.

For example, when I do corporate improv events, I joke about the company's competitor, which always gets a huge laugh. I know this works because it's a subject that is in their wheelhouse, but it's also the opposite (comedy trick!) company that they focus on every day- their competitor. If I made a joke about a brand that I liked that had nothing to do with their industry, it would fall to dead silence. I would have to use the Rule of Threes or Rule of Infinite technique to try to save the joke, but why do all that work when I can just know my audience and hit with a joke on the first try? So we always want to be aware of the people we're talking to so that they can receive our funny jokes that come out of our mouths.

However, there's another way to make comedy less subjective: to connect it to universal truths that basically anyone can relate to. Most people have been in a relationship at one point I their life. Most people have had a day job. Most people have had to sit through traffic while driving somewhere they had to be at a certain time.

Thinking of universal truths to make jokes about will raise your chances of getting a laugh because people can connect to the source material, which is why so many comedians talk about relationships or work. These subjects create a base reality and a great jumping-off point to add their unique point of view that someone might find funny.

But even using these subjects, we can take it one step further by connecting it to Emotions (there's that word again that we talked about all throughout this book and when using the Improv Mindset). Making a joke about the DMV isn't necessarily funny by itself, but if we add in an emotional point of view such as 'standing in a long line, but really needing to use the bathroom and the mind-quarrel between should you leave the line to relieve yourself, or stick it out because you're almost to the front' is a universal emotion that more people will find humorous. Also, to break down this example even further, setting the base reality as the DMV, an opposite thought is needing to go to the bathroom at the DMV, which makes this scenario more comedic than just standing in line and waiting.

So to review, while comedy overall is subjective, we can strengthen our communicability by using universal emotions and opposites to relate to more people who are listening to our comedy, whether it be to a sold out crowd at Madison Square Garden, or just talking to one person during a job interview. But again, improv doesn't have to be funny...unless you want it to be!

CHAPTER 10
LONG FORM IMPROV

To me, the greatest, most mind-blowing impressiveness from improv doesn't necessarily come from individual scenes, but it exists in the result that happens when we put together everything we've been learning in this improv journey up until now- called Long Form.

Long Form improv is when performers get only one suggestion from the audience at the show's beginning, and then improvise for anywhere from 15-60 minutes worth of scenes that resemble a stage play or movie, but all made up on the spot.

This also refers to the long form structure an improv group decides to do. There are many, many, many long forms. If you've ever seen a long form improv show, chances are it was decided beforehand which form the improvisers would be doing that night, such as performing a Harold, an Armando, a Deconstruction, or a Montage.

However, if you saw an improv show that constantly asked the crowd for suggestions and played games, that is known as Short Form improv. In short form, none of the scenes or games the performers play are connected or linked and are completely stand-alone. It's more audience interactive and less like a theatrical piece. The program *Whose Line Is It Anyway* performs short form, and while neither is inherently better than the other, they both use improv in similar ways, and like a lot of things in this book, the more tools you have the better, so learn both. Little may you realize, but a lot of the exercises and warmups in this book have been short form improv games themselves. *Gotcha!*

To me, long form uses more focus and skills since we are creating a world with the piece. The loose structure of the form gives a roadmap of how the storytelling and scene order might happen during the show, and while it's decided which one to perform beforehand, none of these scenes, characters, ideas, or anything else is pre-planned. Just as during a football game, there is a structure of quarters and how long each runs for any other rules- everything that happens is still improvised in the moment.

No matter which structure is decided, long form improv creates a world that the improvisers get to explore and build. Everything in that piece is important as the group is basically creating all the rules, characters, settings, and everything else within this fabricated world. When an improviser is on the sidelines, not performing on stage, they are watching the current scene looking for inspiration on how to expand the world and story...everyone performing is the show's writer, director, actor, set designer, music department, editor, costume designer...everything, all in the moment.

While this may be interesting information, you may be wondering how it all applies to you, the non-performer who wants improv skills for other places in life and never on stage. Well, how an improvised long form operates is equivalent to any of our improv scenarios or conversations. Both start with basically nothing, run for a certain amount of time, and weave in and out, creating the rules for that interaction in the moment.

Think back to the last good conversation you had, maybe with a good friend or relative. Remember all the topics covered in it, the highs and lows, how subjects come back around, and one thing flowed into the next? Well, that is exactly how a good long form piece goes too. So practicing how to pilot long form improv, even if you're never going to perform one on stage, will make you that much more aware and skilled at handling conversations. Cool, right?

Techniques to Use

So far, all the lessons and approaches we've covered are mostly for single, specific subjects: improv rules, the Four Pillars, initiating, etc. All of that should still be applied here, but when you have multiple topics going at at once, there are some techniques improvisers use for long form performances that we can also use that give us specific paths to follow along the way. The following techniques are in no particular order and can be used equally for a subject another person brings up or for one you want to talk about as well.

Explore

To explore a topic means thinking about what else surrounds that topic. Just like explorers *explore*, do that with the subject. Look around and see what other interesting things you can find around that idea. Instead of taking a subject at face value, expand it. Beyond using CREW (which you can also do), you can also think about *Who, What, Where, Why, When, and How* questions here. For example:

Subject: **Dinner Rolls**

> **Who**: Is there a specific baker who only makes this kind of bread?
> **What:** What would be the difference between a dinner roll and, say, late-lunch roll?
> **Where:** Before they are caught in the wild, where do dinner rolls live?
> **Why:** Can a hamburger bun be considered a dinner roll? Why not?
> **When:** When was the first dinner roll invented...or was it discovered?
> **How:** How many dinner rolls can you eat in one sitting?

Obviously, these aren't questions we believe are factual...it's all pretend and play and have fun. Instead of talking serious questions, which is pretty boring, have fun with them- we are doing improv, you know.

Another way to Explore is using our previous concept/exercise called Zoomies. Move outwards or inwards to the subject and explore what you could find there. Does butter create tiny, temporary bread civilizations living once spread onto a dinner roll (zooming in), or what type of restaurant would you find dinner rolls in (zooming out)?

All of these exploring techniques will expand upon the original subject in a much more creative way while we are still simply *Yes, Anding* the original idea brought up.

Heighten

Going hand-in-hand with Explore is also the skill of Heightening. With this, we want to heighten or amplify, the subject or situation talked about to more ridiculous circumstances. Using the dinner roll subject again, we may explore where unused dinner rolls go if not eaten, and then can heighten it by saying they are thrown into a landfill only to soon grow into a sentient dinner roll monster, who can walk and communicate. We could then continue exploring and heightening this- now there is an army of bread monsters (explore), and they are conquering countries around the globe (heighten).

Mostly every comedy uses this technique as it gives funnier ideas from starting with even the drollest places- such as dinner rolls. But instead of thinking, "Oh geez, how am I going to keep this conversation going now that we're on dinner rolls?" we can use heightening to make any subject interesting, fun, and definitely more memorable. Explore and Heighten also work for a character or person mentioned, any location, story, or anything! And remember, use that CREW to Heighten and Explore characters too- wow, we already have so much to work with!

If This is True, What Else is True

This is a great tool to heighten ideas in improvisation. Basically, it is a mental game where we take a fairly small idea and ponder how that could ripple out to become a bigger idea (also called *If, Then* for short). We ask "if this fact is true, then what else *could* also be true?"

Here's an example. Let's say someone says, "I don't really like dinner rolls." At face value, there's not much there and you will probably get a response such as, "What? Really? How can you not like dinner rolls?" or "Oh that's weird, I love them." Both of which aren't really helpful responses to move the communication forward – the first being a question and the second only being about yourself.

But if we *If, Then* the fact that someone doesn't like dinner rolls, then it *could* be true that millions of people don't like them either, and if that's true, then it could be true that somewhere right now, the heads of all the major dinner roll companies are brainstorming ways to still make a profit with their bread ingredients. Now, if *that* is true, then it could be true that there's a new perfume on the market: Buttery Bread, the newest fragrance from Chanel.

See? By using *If, Then* it causes us to reach new, fun ideas from even the simplest of statements. Open your imagination and try it- it's fun.

Find Similarities...or Differences

Another thing we can do is find similarities, or differences, within ourselves to something the other person is saying. As we said in the *Matching* techniques, when someone else starts an interaction, people like to be around people who we are alike, so talking to someone, exploring and getting to know them can really just come down to searching for something we have in common. This is the ultimate *Yes, And* as we are literally agreeing to what the other person said and getting on the same page, like we are now.[44]

Think about a time you met a stranger and how the energy of the interaction changed once you found out you had something in common. "You know so-and-so too? Oh my goodness, small world!" It immediately becomes lighter as we feel safer to this other human with whom we have some commonality. It already feels like you're friends!

On the flip side of this, we can also find differences with the other person. Again, people like to communicate with others that are like them, so tread lightly here. If we keep forcing our opposing views and ideas on the other person, they probably won't want to keep talking to us, or worse, tell others how bad it was and not do it either.

But, we don't have to agree on everything. Part of what makes humans instating is that we're the same species, but no two of us are exactly the same. It's okay to share our opinion on why we might not like something the other person does, as long as we back it up with our Why. If we just say how something they like is "dumb and stupid...because it is." we're just being a jerk. But if we share that we can't get into a certain movie, for example, share why not. It continues the conversation and allows you both to discuss your likes and dislikes.

Again, we want to keep the idea of Yes, And going, so be sure we agree on the topic and adding what we like or dislike about it, while keeping an open mind to see where the other person is coming from, even if you don't agree. This can even lead to more topics of discussion by *exploring* their reasons.

---

[44] Page because it's a book. Yes, that's right, I do comedy.

PERSON 1: *Dinner rolls are the worst food ever. They always make me sick!*
PERSON 2: *Maybe you have a gluten allergy.*
PERSON 1: *Oh, I never got tested for something like that. Could that be it?*

Stay open minded, listen, and share your thoughts while stating interest in the other person, and you'll keep this conversation going so long that you might even find a new best friend.

Linear Continuations

In this method, the first topic brought up inspires the next and continues forward directly inspired by the topic that preceded it, exploring and heightening the ideas and people mentioned in a linear way.

When you feel like you have exhausted a subject, there are a few things we can do to create a new subject to start exploring and talking about. *Any* of the Initiation techniques we've learned will work here to get us inspired by something that was just mentioned.

PERSON 1: *...so I ate so many dinner rolls yesterday that it made me sick.*
PERSON 2: (using a *word* from that sentence) *Oh no! Have you ever eaten so much food at a Thanksgiving that you start to get sick when it turns November 1st?*

In addition to all those ways to initiate (take your pick), you can also *word associate* something that was said.

PERSON 1: *...so I ate so many dinner rolls yesterday that it made me sick.*
PERSON 2: *Oh no! Speaking of rolls, I got a new foam roller, and it's a miracle for my sore legs.*

Dinner Rolls led to *Foam Roller*. You get it. And while that example shows Person 2 not really responding to what Person 1 said, it's an example of how to never run out of stuff to say. We still want to listen and respond to what people say to us instead of, "OK, my turn to talk!" It once again goes back to having to listen. Most of the time, we reach that awkward silence in our interactions because someone stopped listening to the other person, and we feel like there's nothing else to go off of. But by listening, it's impossible not to be inspired! So get out of your head and into the moment.

Multiple Threads

This version is just as it sounds – where multiple, completely unrelated subjects were directly or indirectly inspired by the first topic, or suggestion, being explored at once and we move back and forth between them.

A subject comes up, and it inspires a tangent that is then followed and expanded on, but we still have that original subject that wasn't fully completed. What normally happens is someone starts to tell a story and it makes the other person think of another story from their own experience. They cut off the first person to tell their story, and we never go back to the original one. But if we are paying attention enough, and not trying to just force our own agenda, it's perfectly fine to take a tangent, as long as we remember to go back. "Anyway, back to what you were saying about [whatever]."

When we move between stories, the topics of discussion seem endless! This is when we might feel that our conversation is flowing really well and we have so much stuff to talk about. While there can be infinite tangents, and you know how much I've said that the infinite is not always our friend, it's best to focus on three or four only. More than some things will be forgotten, but by keeping them to a few, you and maybe even the other person can move more easily between the threads.

When you are inspired to hear more about another subject, the best way to do this is to follow it and build off of it like you do in any previous methods. Then when you feel like you have reached a natural stopping point in that subject, go back to another one and do the same. Then repeat the process, going back-and-forth between each story or whatever the stories may have grown into,

This Multiple Thread method is more memorable by crossing over storylines, meaning that a person, place, object, or theme from one storyline connects to another. For example:

Subject 1: Dog had to go to the vet for check-up.

Subject 2: Bought a bunch of dinner rolls at the store that tasted weird.

Subject 3: A new assignment at work has been challenging and exciting.

So as you both talk about the dog, then about the veggies, and then work, and back to veggies, and the dog (all in any order), you may see a natural connection between them. Some examples could be:

Connection: *It seems like those dinner rolls need to get a check-up too.*

Connection: *The dog may have been sick due to eating someof those dinner rolls that dropped on the floor.*

Connection: *Your next assignment might be what's wrong with bread right now.*

Connection: *I wonder if a veterinarian right now is hoping for a new assignment other than doing routine pet check-ups. Someone brings in a cool animal, like an alligator.*

Again, these are just some examples. The more we listen and take in what is being said, the easier it will be to see the connections.

Now, connections are very fun and gratifying, but a word of warning. If you crossover stories too soon, they will seem forced and almost look like the only reason you wanted to know more about something was to connect it, and that you weren't interested in what the other person had to say. So tread lightly and wait a little bit before connecting. Connections like these, just as stories crossover in some TV shows, usually put a close to the conversation, or at least the subject threads being talked about. So it's suggested that as you listen, build threads, and discover connections, you don't say them right when you notice them. Keep them in your mind and wait for the right moment, usually when there is a lull, or you feel the current topic of conversation may be winding down.

If we build these multiple threads and are patient with the connections and time them well, we will get a laugh or at least have a memorable interaction with the other person. Again, it comes down to rule number one, listening.

Callbacks

A reason why connection story threads works so well is because it's a form of a callback. In comedy, a callback refers to something that has already been established or talked about, but is not being focused on at this moment or at all. It's something that everyone *was aware* of in the interaction, but now we're onto a different topic. But by bringing calling something back, it works as an inside joke between the people since you both know the reference.

Callbacks work best, like connections, when the subject is seemingly forgotten about. If you callback something that was just said, it seems like you are a little slow on the uptake, "Why are we talking about that again?" But wait it out until the idea seems long forgotten, and a callback is sure to get a good response.

Unlike connecting threads, a callback doesn't have to connect two ideas and can be anything that was previously said- a person, location, word, etc. Using the subject examples above of vegetables that tasted weird, maybe at some point in the conversation, you or someone else excuses themselves to use the restroom. You could say, "They probably had some vegetables that tasted weird." which would make everyone laugh, because, one, you weren't talking about that anymore, and two, it connected a subject to the present moment.

If we take the idea of Yes, And, which says that anything said is true, then it would mean if there were vegetables that tasted weird, even if the person said they had them a month ago, then it means that yes, those vegetables exist in the world, and maybe the person has to go to the restroom because of them.

This is just one example, and there are many that we can take from the interaction. Anything that was previously said can be brought back. Just like we love catchphrases that people or characters on TV say, the same goes for callbacks.

One more thing while we're on the subject of callbacks- just as there is no wrong answer in improv, *any* callback can work. Let's say we make a callback to something, and it falls flat- no one laughs or gets what we are referring to. Instead of trying to explain it, "Remember, because we talked about vegetables like 20 minutes ago?" just let it land flat and move on. Then, a few minutes later, when the opportunity for a callback presents itself, say the same callback again. It may work here, but if it doesn't, repeat the process until it does.

This takes a lot of bravery to repeat a joke that didn't work, but it's all in how we do it. You have to be self-aware that you are, indeed, repeating a callback joke. You aren't saying it again as if it was the first time. So maybe say it a little bit more sarcastically, or a little too excited about it, or that you think it's hilarious. You just don't want to do it with the emotion of "no one heard me the first time, so I'm desperately trying again." Have more fun with it, and keep doing it until it works.... because it will, *eventually*. Repeating this callback, which can be done for those who worked and those who didn't, will get a laugh.[45]

Telling Stories

Any live theatre performance or movie we go to see has a beginning, middle, and end and follows characters throughout, expanding the world they live in, and watching how they deal with specific situations. (hmm, sounds like the goal of long form improv, does it not?) So, you can use the techniques of storytelling in improv in your everyday life too.

If you feel like someone who isn't good at telling stories, here might be why. If a story is subject after subject and meanders or doesn't give enough context (aka CREW), it's hard to follow or be captivated about what's going on.

Stories work when we have developed the characters and relationships. We want to connect to the people or events in a story - individuals dealing with problems that break the routine of everyday life, and go along to ride as the story heightens and imagine what we would do in the same circumstances.

Looking for individual jokes and punchlines doesn't make a good story. Jokes work *within* the story. Just imagine how boring a television show would be if the characters never did anything but sat around making jokes and acting weirder and weirder in every scene they did. No one would care. But those same characters doing that in a world where there was a zombie outbreak, or they were running a bar, or trying to live their adult lives gives us shows like " *Walking Dead*," "*Always Sunny in Philadelphia*,"

---

[45] See chapter on Comedy for *Rule of Three, Rule of Infinite*

and "*Friends.*" (yes, even "*Seinfeld*" a 'show about nothing" had the characters follow a story in each episode). They all have story and so should you!

Outside of having defined CREW for pieces of the story, how do we actually tell it? There are many theories on how to tell a story; from Joseph Campbell's Hero's Journey to the common screenwriting Three-Act Structure, the number of books on the subject of Storytelling seems endless. But the version I found the clearest and most helpful is based on Aristotle's Poetics, which says every story has five simple elements.

Balance, Unbalance, Quest, Climax, New Balance.

Look at every story, movie, or narrative that exists, and we will find that it follows the same structure. Every. Single. One. So let's break them down.

Balance: this is the setup of the world. We are introduced to our characters and see their everyday life; nothing exciting happens outside their normal daily routines.

Unbalance: uh oh... something came into their life that wasn't there before and completely messes with that previous routine we saw in the Balance. Now they must take action as a result of this Unbalance to try to put things back to normal. This is commonly called the Inciting Incident.

Quest: this is the meatiest part of the story as it shows our characters from the Balance going on a journey to solve the problem that occurred in the Unbalance. Usually, we try to find the easiest solution, and when that doesn't work, the Quest goes deeper as we look for other options.

Climax: everything has led up to this moment. This is when our characters will either perish or triumph. We all know climaxes, as they are the most exciting parts of every movie we've ever seen.

New Balance: after the hair-raising moments of the Climax, we now see the results of that event. This is where we get to see our character's life now that their Journey has come to a close. Usually, they are changed in some way or learned a lesson, but also, sometimes, they're right back to where they started (which happens in most TV sitcoms). This is called the New Balance because it literally resets their world to their new everyday life, and they live on until a new Unbalance occurs, which starts a new story. This is sometimes also called the epilogue.

Sounds pretty epic right? Well, it works for those epic stories like *Star Wars* or *Lord of the Rings*, but also smaller stories in our lives too. Here's an example:

> <u>Balance</u>: Alex is home with no plans.
> <u>Unbalance</u>: Alex gets invited to a dinner party and told to bring dinner rolls
> <u>Quest</u>: Alex must go shopping for rolls, which means choosing which store to go to, driving there, picking what rolls to buy- pre-made or from scratch, etc.
> <u>Climax</u>: Alex finds the perfect dinner roll recipe and makes them for the party.
> <u>New Balance</u>: Alex is now really good at making dinner rolls.

Now, this doesn't mean that the story you tell will only be five sentences because that would be boring. Use as many as you need to tell the story, with the Quest being the largest part. Let us know who the characters are and what they were doing before anything different happened, and then let's all relive the journey together using these Five Elements.

There you go. Following this easy structure will make your stories more enjoyable for anyone listening. Story structure in a very easily digestible few pages; no need to scour blogs and books anymore.

It's About Now

Wow, there we have a lot of different techniques to weave in and out of the interacting we may find ourselves in. The biggest takeaway here is that you are creating something original to this moment. Not just a collection of one-line jokes and not even a collection of just random subjects. But an entire piece. If there was a courtroom stenographer[46] writing down everything said in the conversation, at the end we should be able to stand back from it and see a beautiful work of art- subjects and ideas flowing back and forth and connecting.

Your goal shouldn't be to just 'chat,' but to build something with an end result that looks like the interaction was all fully planned and pre-written. Improv is an amazing art form that can help you achieve this. The best thing we could ever hear after an interaction is that it flowed well and was interesting and memorable. If you use these methods, you can help any conversation look like it wasn't improvised on the spot; that's pure magic! Again, it's not worrying about having to come up with witty ideas, but just listening and building off of what is laid right in front of us by the other person...and/or sharing our ideas in focused ways.

---

[46] Is this job still a thing, or are robots doing it by now?

EXERCISE: The Montage

The Montage is a freeform style of improv where anything goes and builds what ends up looking like an improvised play or TV show. But you can use the same concept in telling stories in life without ever having to get on a stage.

IMPROV EXERCISE

THE MONTAGE

How to Do It:

01 Take a piece of paper write down a random word at the top.

02 Below it, come up with as many ideas you can think of inspired from that word. These could be memories, objects or people related to the subject, situations, jokes, anecdotes, stories from your own experience...as many ideas as you can!

03 Look back at the list and see how you can connect some of the ideas and build new ideas off of what you already wrote down using the "If, Then" technique

Skills Used: Building Ideas & Storytelling

Montage Example: *Airplane* **is the suggestion**

Original Ideas:

- crowded tight spaces
- peanuts, pretzels, water
- small TV
- security check
- turbulence
- trying to sleep in a weird position
- crying baby
- crying adult

If, Then Ideas:

- a movie theater that is filled with as many people as possible but has a tiny screen
- a crying pilot on a plane
- someone who likes sleeping in an uncomfortable position
- a restaurant that gives you airplane food only
- a theme park ride that recreates the airline flying experience, but nothing more.

The **goal** of this exercise is to show you how many ideas you can create just by using one word as a jumping off point. Using this, it's impossible for you to "go blank" ever again!

The same exercise can be used if you are trying to brainstorm a new idea or product, as it's a great way to build new ideas off of things related to the subject matter.

CHAPTER 11
REAL-LIFE SCENARIOS

Until now in our reading, we've worked on different skills that we can use for any improv scenario we may find ourselves in. Now, there are unlimited combinations of unique events you may come across, but we're going to go through some specific examples to help you handle the situations better next time. The upcoming information isn't supposed to represent the be-all-and-end-all of how to handle these events- there are plenty of other resources written in depth about each of them- but we're going to look at them directly from an improv approach. The scenarios listed in this chapter are also the most common ones students bring up when taking my classes, but even if you've never had to deal with these, at some point, you may just discover you end up in one and now will have some tricks up your sleeve – unless you are wearing a short-sleeved shirt, then maybe the tricks are just in your pocket.

I'm also going to give some short example stories from when I used improv techniques when I was in some of the same situations in real life myself. Hopefully, it will show you that they are helpful and that I am talking-the-talk from what we've already gone over!

Before we go on, here's a tip that you can use that applies to all of the following situations: for each of these scenarios, imagine you are doing an improv scene or exercise (like we've done already in the book, and that you were just playing a character who is in that situation. Most likely, when you've done one of the exercises, you weren't nervous or weren't sure what to say because you were just playing and having fun. So bring that same energy to these scenarios! Again, nobody knows what's going to happen, and nobody has a script, and everyone is improvising all the time. So instead of practicing your improv and then getting "real serious" for these situations, treat them as if they are an improv in themselves where you just so happen to be playing yourself in the situation, and instead of your emotion being nervous, why not make it confident and fun?

Job Interview

If you've never had to be in a job scenario situation before, lucky you. However, most of us have, and from experience, we can tell you that it's one of the most awkward and uncomfortable situations as there's a lot of pressure and a lot on the line- getting the job and thus getting paid- so it makes it even harder to fully be your best self.

While you can prepare a lot before you ever step into the room with the interviewer- such as knowing what the job entails, the company's history and plans, having your materials such as resume or letters of reference updated, polished, and ready to hand over, and doing an online search for common interview questions- you still cannot be completely secure on what's going to fully happen in the meeting, which really does make it a perfect place to use your new improv skills.

One might think that a job interview is all about you talking and telling as many facts about yourself as possible to impress the other person, but that isn't really true and will make you seem desperate and not someone people would want to be around. Outside of a company wanting to hire someone qualified for the position, among many other boxes to check off- some that there's no way of knowing- you also want to make a good connection with the person interviewing you. You want to show them that you're not just some crazy person who saw the "Help Wanted" sign and just wandered in and not someone they're going to regret being stuck working with every day. Yes, you will have to talk about your skills, but you also want to show your personality and that you are fun to be around.

Some of the skills we've already used that can be applied here are *Listening* and *Matching*. You really want to listen to hear what the person is saying so you can convey your information in a way that meets what they need. For example, if the interviewer says how they need dependable people, now wouldn't be the time to bring up the 'fun" story of when your car broke down a few months ago. I'm not saying that you lie to them, but there's no reason to bring up a negative thing that happened in the past, especially if it doesn't apply to what you were going to provide to them in the future...and if they didn't even ask.

Also, it's a good idea to match the other person's energy. So, you definitely should convey confidence. You don't want to convey *cockiness,* which shows that you have an ego and might be hard to work with. In improv words, pretend the interviewer has initiated this improv scene, and you are *matching* them and are going to respond. The easy thing here is you already know all the information because you did your research about the job and know yourself beforehand, so you do not have to come up with new stuff randomly in the moment. As we discussed previously, matching puts you on the same page as the other person and makes you someone they could be comfortable with.

I remember some years ago that I was applying for a job at a Chicago themed pizza place- that was not in Chicago whatsoever, but it seemed to work until, I think, the entire chain filed for bankruptcy years later. Anyway... one of the reasons I wanted to work there, outside of needing a job, was that they mainly played one of my favorite genres of music, Chicago Blues. I thought if I was going to work in a restaurant multiple days a week, at least I would enjoy the music.

By listening and assuming during the interview, I could tell that most of the other staff were a fun group of people (phrases such as "like a family" and "all friends here" are clues). Well, inevitably, during the meeting, the person across the table asked me the common question, "Why do you want to work here?" and instead of giving a canned answer of what probably most people said, such as, "I really appreciate what the company does, etc." I said, with a smile on my face, "Well, honestly, I really like the music you play. Do you curate the songs yourself? If not, is it possible to apply for that job instead?" They replied with confusion at first, then laughed once they saw I was joking.

The interview continued as normal, looking at my experience and availability, etc., and they offered me the job. Now was it because of my random joke? Who's to say? But it didn't hurt. I showed that I was fun to be around, while the rest of the interview was professional, and not someone that no one would want to work with. (also, I was offered a serving job, not a music curator, unfortunately).

So be present in your next interview and know that you prepared as much as you can, and everything else is up to your improv skills. It doesn't mean you're guaranteed to get it, but it will be one extra advantage you have over other people who go in and never connect with the person they're talking to. But you know better.

Dating

If there's one thing that's more awkward than a job interview, it would have to be dating. While the former is all about hiring someone to work with, dating has much more of an intimate goal. Plus, more emotions are involved, physically and mentally, which really makes things more awkward. In addition, what may be pretty obvious the some, but took me a while to understand, is that some people go on dates for different reasons and different goals for what they want out of the date- some are looking for a serious long-term relationship, while others are just looking for a relationship tonight. So a lot is going on when it comes to dating. But whatever the reason you may have to go on a date, we are all trying to impress the other person. Yet, doing so requires more than your favorite button-down shirt or favorite top. We want to show our full best self in hopes of being a match with the person we're on the date with.

Side note, it really amazes me that even for first dates, some people still can't be on their best behavior. It's one time, for a few hours, but they're still people who end up showing their worst qualities. It amazes me. On that, I want to be very clear that with any of these scenarios, especially dating, I don't want anyone to try to use improv to lie or be someone they're not. It's the contrary; I want you to be more of yourself and highlight your best qualities because that's really what people want to see.

The Improv skills to use while going on a date overlap pretty well with our job interview skills. You want to listen to the other person to build the conversation, create rapport, and find out what you both have in common. Again, people like people they are like. Even so, sometimes, no matter how good another person might sound on paper, the chemistry just doesn't work out, and there's nothing to be done about it. In times like this, you can't take it personally, but if you know that you did all you could to show your best qualities and be your most charming self, it will make it easier not to have any regrets. So that's why listening is important when you're on a date.

When it feels like we are listened to and heard, it automatically creates a connection with another human being. We've all been in situations, and maybe even dates, where the other person just rattled on and on and talked as if we weren't even there. I can guarantee you probably didn't have a second date with that person. So listen to what the person has to say, be interested in them, and find commonalities while they're talking. It's pretty much *Yes, And* 101, folks.

Also similar to job interviews is matching. Match the other person's energy; match how they feel about the situation and location and conversation topics. Matching allows you to get on the same page regarding what they're comfortable with. Sometimes other people take more time to open up to someone, and I mean that physically too, and that's something to be aware of so you don't come off pushy. By matching and listening to the other person, you won't put them in an uncomfortable situation, which you should never ever do under any circumstances, date or not.

So outside of listening, matching, and using any and all of the skills for conversation (such as CREW and Long Form), another really good improv quality to bring into your dating life is having fun. While job interviews and dating are similar, you don't want a date to feel like a job interview where one person is just asking a bunch of questions while the other person is giving answers. (I can tell you from personal experience that I've done this at least on one occasion, and for sure, it wasn't very fun, and there definitely wasn't the second date. But more about me in a little bit.) So just like one of our improv rules, don't ask a bunch of questions. It's okay to ask some questions to get to know the other person, but if it's just question after question, it will not be an exciting date.

Then how do you bring fun into one of the most awkward things we do as humans? Well, it goes back to literally chapter 1 of this book. Most people are afraid of looking stupid and embarrassing themselves, but again, if you put yourself out there, be vulnerable, and don't take yourself so seriously, you can have more fun. Play, be silly, and make jokes- whether they're good or not. If you have a smile on your face and you're having fun, even lame jokes can be fun! (Think of all the puns and dad jokes that exist. Said seriously from a literal dad isn't usually funny. But said in an ironic way and with a sense of joy behind it, they actually are pretty enjoyable and funny.)

From my own experience, I was a pretty late bloomer in terms of dating- I never knew how people could be so vulnerable and charming and go on dates with other people...like what's the secret?! I literally thought I wasn't funny enough or good enough to ever be able to do that. I would think there was some secret that you had to know, and I read many terrible books in search of finding it too. But then, when I started to be more of myself- which I equate to the person you are when you're most relaxed around your favorite people while hanging out in a casual setting- I found that I had no trouble meeting people. When I stopped trying to figure out how everybody else was doing it and what I was doing wrong, and just played, had fun, and was my silly self, everything started coming together. They say to be yourself, but really what you want to be *is the best version of* yourself.

Really, for every section in this chapter, having fun and not taking things so seriously will be useful. Like we said before, being around someone who is an energy drag and takes everything so heavy is not fun. There's too much serious and heavy stuff everywhere else, so when we're doing something for recreation or social purposes, we thirst for experiences to be more fun. So instead of thinking you aren't enough, or you aren't sure what to do, just play and have fun as if you were hanging out with your best friends, even though the person sitting across from you is basically a stranger. But if all goes well, they may not be strangers anymore.

Work Meetings

While most meetings really could just be an email- because wow, is it ever frustrating to sit through a long meeting for basically someone to just hear the sound of their own voice talk for something that could have been sent in writing- we're going to talk about the kind of meetings where interaction is not only welcome but could be an advantage for you as well.

In a lot of work meetings, it's easy to zone out and be there, so you are only counted as presented and not reprimanded- especially with more and more meetings being done virtually, it's even easier to pretend you're paying attention when really you're just doing something else on your computer. But that would really be the biggest waste of time, which is probably why we feel like a lot of meetings are a waste because we don't *want* to be there. Instead, what if you were to use that scheduled work meeting, even for something boring, as an opportunity to practice your improv skills? You might actually find that you, dare I say, enjoy them.

To do this, you can probably guess what my first suggestion is going to be. Listening. Just as listening is an important skill to use in every other scenario we discussed, it can also assist you in meetings. Listening is the number one rule of improv because it is the most important thing to do in any improv situation. Listening, even if you don't have any ideas or anything to contribute preconceived in your head, allows your mind to create ideas and make connections that you probably wouldn't have gotten if you were thinking about how much longer until lunch. So as I've said it many times before, listen, listen, listen. You hear me?

Listening also helps you know when to speak up during the meeting. Sometimes there are so many people that you feel like you can never get a word it. Simply by listening, you can sort of get the rhythm and flow of the conversation and know when to jump in so you can share your opinion and thoughts as well. A good way to do this is the use of transitional words to set up that you are about to talk. Starting your sentence with something like, "Yes..." or "Definitely..." or "So..." or "That's great...." or "I got it! What if..." or even literally saying "Yes, and..." all set up that you have something to say and signals everyone else to listen. It may not always work, as some people just talk over others, but it will give you the best chance of sharing your good thoughts too.[47]

With that, you can also use another improv skill of Assuming. Assuming allows getting your mind to connect to ways to solve problems faster than anyone else. If you listen and hear that there's a problem going on, you can assume there's more information and maybe be able to jump to conclusions faster. For example, a problem about social media not reaching enough people. Maybe you could assume that the time of posts is bad, or the content needs changing, instead of just trying to post more and more of the same content that hasn't been working.

However, if I was to choose the number one improv skill to be used in meetings, it would be Yes, And. You've probably been in multiple meetings with someone who is a Yes, But type of person. They probably read somewhere that it is helpful to agree with other people in meetings because it allows things to move forward, but they still say that dreaded

---

[47] see the chapter on difficult people for more help.

But at the end of the sentence. Something like, "I hear what you are suggesting, BUT...we're still going to do it my way." Again, this is all about their fear of letting go of control. It's an ego move. They think they can do things better because they are in charge, so no matter what anybody else suggests, they're going to shoot it down and force their ideas.

But as we already learned, agreeing *and* building off of other people is truly the best way to come up with better ideas that we would have never thought of on your own. So if there's something that has to be figured out, or solved, or a new idea to come up within a meeting, Yes, And is the way to go.

Even if you are the person leading the meeting, you might be in charge, but it doesn't mean you have all of the answers. You have a much higher chance of reaching a good outcome if you Yes, And every idea that comes up and see where it leads you. Even if you Yes, And for an hour and it leads you to a dead end, you can always start again. But on the flip side, it might lead you to a new idea that's actually better than any that any individual could have come up with on your own. While not Yes, Anding, you *could* also end up there, sure, but your chances are much greater if everybody works together in build off of each other's ideas.

A story I will share about using improv in meetings didn't actually happen to me, but to one of my former students. I'm not going to say their name or any other specifics that give away what they were working on- you'll just have to fill in the blanks for yourself.

So one of my former students was studying improv with me because they were shy and didn't know how to speak up during production meetings. You see, they were a crew member for a big-budget film production and felt that their title was too low compared to everyone around them, so they never spoke up.

Well, there was one important meeting happening that would decide the look of a specific character in this huge, blockbuster movie, and everyone was tossing around ideas. So far, none of them were working, but then the student had an idea. Now, normally, they would keep their mouths shut and just wait for somebody else to come up with an answer as had always happened before, but since they were taking an improv class, they decided to speak up. They shared their idea with the group, and it turns out not only did the big name director like it so much that it was used in the final movie as well as all of the marketing and what you probably picture when you hear the name of this movie featuring tall, lanky blue aliens[48], but they also got a promotion to a more creative role.

Suffice to say, this former student now lives in a beautiful, expansive penthouse downtown. They could have easily kept quiet and stayed in their comfort zone, but they decided to take a leap and look where it led them.[49]

So the next time you're in a boring ol' meeting, why not try to make the most of it? You never know where it might lead.

Presentation or Pitch

Unlike a standard work meeting, this category covers when you have to prepare a presentation or pitch and deliver it to a group of people. The easy thing about this improv scenario is you really get to fully prepare what you're going to say. You already know what the subject will be, and

---

[48] That's not too specific right? Oops!
[49] P.S., can I get a cut?

you could do as much research, planning, and losing sleep the night before as you want. Yet sometimes, we still get nervous.

This is most likely because of the fear of public speaking. Most people would rather die than have to public speak- which is an insane fact from some survey. But it's not the actual act of speaking that makes us nervous. It's that we may come across as someone who doesn't know what we're talking about. That and deity forbid someone should ask us a question that we didn't already have her prepared answered for, and it throws off your entire presentation and makes you look like a fool.

Well, we already talked about not letting the fear of looking stupid stop you, so I'm not going to repeat all of that now, although it all applies. Being afraid to talk in front of people is only natural because it's unnatural. Unless you grew up in a household where you had lots of practice speaking in front of large groups, it's probably difficult for you. If humans were meant to always speak in front people, our mouths would be shaped like megaphones. (Picture it, the image in my head is pretty funny). However, we still find ourselves in situations where we have to give presentations. Work presentations, a speech at a wedding, a eulogy, or even a short speech after receiving a gift- everyone wanting us to stand up and talk! But knowing that the situation *will* happen at some point, and that you probably will be nervous, is actually helpful. Being aware that you're going to be nervous is better than suddenly being nervous. At least the other one you knew was going to come on. And really, nervousness is just an emotion that is negatively labeled.

Think about it. Imagine two people are in line to go on a roller coaster. One person is excited and they say, "Oh, I'm so excited, I have butterflies in my stomach." While another person is nervous, and they say, "Oh, I'm so nervous, I have butterflies in my stomach." It's the exact same feeling, it's just how we label them. So instead of saying that you are nervous about your presentation, tell yourself that you are excited. It tricks your mind into thinking that the feeling isn't all that bad.

Here's also something that helped me overcome stage fright at the beginning of my performing career. Everyone is expecting you to be up there presenting. If you are on a stage or in front of the room speaking, everyone in attendance assumes that you are supposed to be doing that. If you were to stand up in the middle of a restaurant and start giving a presentation, that would be more nerve-racking because no one is predicting that would happen and there's more of a chance for them to yell at you to sit down. But if you have a scheduled presentation, everyone is thus assuming there will be a presentation by you. No one is expecting you to be bad. They're just expecting there to be a presentation. So why be nervous about something expected? If you look at it from this perspective, it can help you a little to get over those public speaking nerves.

Okay, so you prepared your presentation, practiced memorizing your word-for-word talk many times, and feel pretty comfortable with it, but then somebody asks you a question or something else happens that you didn't plan for. Before you run out the door hiding your face, why not enact those hot new improv skills?

Outside of listening and responding, you can *Yes, And* what just came up and then make light of it with a joke. Just because somebody asked you a question, even if it's a very serious one, doesn't mean you have to answer in a serious tone. The best public speakers do this as well. They get asked a very serious question, and they answer with a smile and a joke before then continuing on with their real answer.

So when an unexpected moment happens in your pre-planned presentation, listen, take a moment, and have fun with the beginning of your response-which will also give you a chance to think of your real answer. You don't have to respond within a second with a real answer, but use the time of the joke, and the hopeful laughter from the joke, to think about what you really want to say.

Another good skill to use, is voice and posture, which aligns with what we talked about with the emotions a bit too. When we're nervous and anxious, we close ourselves off in our physicality- cross our arms and legs, and usually our shoulders slumped and our head down. This isn't how you want to give a presentation, though. So actively changing your emotion from nervous to confident would cause you to stand up straight, head up, arms and legs uncrossed, and make eye contact with people (or you could look at their foreheads if close or just above their heads if farther away if you are still nervous).

Changing your posture will also change your vocal quality. Again, the more nervous we are, the more our voice volume is low and cause us to mumble our words because we don't want anyone to actually hear us. When we're confident, we speak loudly and enunciate our words because we want people to hear what we have to say.

As someone who used to be very nervous, speaking up was the hardest thing for me to do when I had to give presentations and starting in acting. If this is you, a trick to help you is to speak louder than you think you should be speaking. It might feel like yelling, but because you are a soft-spoken person, it will actually just be normal volume. And even if you are speaking a little bit louder than normal, you'll get used to it, and it'll even out to a regular discernible level. Speak up, we want to hear you at this presentation we were all expecting anyway.

In addition to writing this book, I'm also a screenwriter, which means I commonly have to/get to pitch ideas to film and TV studio executives. Many writers don't like pitching- writers usually also mean they are introverts- but I actually enjoy it because I view it as an improv game. I play the character of 'someone good at pitching.'

A few years back, I was giving a pitch to the head of a pretty big mouse-shaped studio, and it was late in the afternoon, so they were pretty burnt out from having meetings with other writers all day. So as I was going along with my pitch, I could tell they weren't paying attention. Instead of just continuing my rehearsed description of my show idea, I switched gears and started making up insane things- stuff like giant amorphous body parts falling from the sky and then sitting down to eat a good Middle Eastern dinner. None of it made sense or was supposed to make any sense, but it got the attention of the person who was not paying any to me and brought them back into focusing on my pitch. They asked me what I was talking about, and they couldn't do any of that stuff for a show, and I said, "Ah ha... I got your attention, though, didn't I?" We both laughed and then I continued my pitch, which went really well. I'd love to tell you that the ending of this story is that the show was picked up and became one of the most popular programs on TV, but honestly, I can't even remember what my original pitch was anyways. But what I do remember is this story during the process of pitching.

So lighten up. Everyone is expecting to see a presentation anyway, so you may as well have the most fun with it.

Random Person

Now, this scenario is where things really are the most unexpected. You're standing in the produce aisle, deciding which avocado you're going to buy, and suddenly, someone comes up and starts talking to you. Yikes!

Usually, this catches us so off guard that we respond with a quick "I don't know" just to get the person away from us, which makes sense! We were probably very much in our heads thinking about something completely different and weren't being present at all, so it would be hard to form a response pretty fast from an unexpected interaction like this.

But again, improv is trying to teach us to be more present and in the moment, which means not being too stuck up in our head to be able to answer a simple question that someone might ask us, even unexpectedly. So the first step in handling a scenario like this is to be more present overall. You can use any of the exercises previously listed about using our presence in addition to, you know, I'm going to say it, *Listen*.

Listen and take in everything around you instead of keeping your mind preoccupied with something you have to do later or something that you did earlier in the day. Notice the sounds and sites around all around. Even if it's a grocery store you've been to a hundred times, there's something always different about it any time you go anywhere if you notice it closely enough. Maybe there's a broken light, or a spill of apples, or at the very least, the people there will be a different combination of shoppers than last time.

Once you're present and someone approaches you with a question or a statement, the next thing to do is to Yes, And them. Just as in an improv scene, if someone initiates first, it means they have something they want to say. So the person coming up to you is talking to you because they need to say *something*. Maybe it's a question about where something is located ("do you know where the exit is?") or your opinion ("Is this cereal any good?") or experience with something ("What did you order to eat? I'm not sure."). Nevertheless, they do have something they feel the need to say so much that they walked over to you to ask. So instead of responding quickly with "I don't know" to get the person to go away, Yes, And what they have to say.

You can do this in any way we've talked about or simply Match them and add your own opinion on the subject. Such as, "You know, I was wondering how to get out of this store too!" or, "I've been buying this same cereal for 10 years, so I'd say it's pretty good." or, "I got the special just because it caught my eye. Seems interesting!"

The truth is that people just want to be heard. Our attention spans have gotten minuscule and there's plenty of things to give our awareness to, so when someone talks to you, smile, make eye contact with them, and hear what they have to say. Even if you can't help them in any way, or even if you don't want to, just being able to be heard might make that person's day. On that, 'making someone's day' seems like a lost deed that doesn't exist anymore. But just by simply doing a kind act of smiling and hearing what someone has to say might make their life just a little better. The people who feel better are also usually a little happier too, and those who are happier tend to do less bad things to people and help others out. Now, if you can make one person's day, it could create a ripple effect that results in more people also being affected in other positive ways. Our world definitely needs a lot more of that these kinds of actions these days. So don't be so quick to brush someone off when they might just have a simple question for you and just want to be heard. It's the least we can do.

Now, with all that said, we usually might brush people off quickly because we fear what they might want from us. Some people might try to interact with you to spill all of their problems, want something from you, trick you into giving them something, or even go somewhere with them. A real concern!

But, if you are present enough, and someone approaches you and asks you a question, you'll be much better at listening to your instincts and knowing whether it's a safe interaction or not. If you feel you might be in danger, in any way, whether it be physical or even just emotional, by someone dumping all of their problems on you, it's okay to shut them down and not continue the interaction. Of course, by all means, be safe above anything else. You can't make someone's day if you are in a bad situation. So, in times like this, it's okay to not Yes, And and not match them and simply say "I don't know" and put yourself in a safer location. ("Yes, you are talking to me, And, I'm going to shut you down.")

Although, even with a denial or saying "I don't know," some people are a little more relentless and can't take social cues such as those and continue their query. You might have found yourself in situations where someone goes on and on and on (and on!) and never give a break in words enough for them to even breathe and give you a polite chance to tell them you have to leave.

In these cases, since they are being rude by not giving you a chance to say anything, it's okay to be a little bit rude as well so you can get out of there. Simply holding up your hand and saying,"Gotta go." Or making a joke, or saying "No thanks." and walking away is fine. Also, you don't have to apologize for leaving. They were the ones who were the "bad improvisers" and not listening to anything that you had to say, so get out of there so you can go create better interactions with other people. If you're a caring person, you might feel guilty for cutting someone, but don't. You don't owe anyone your time and attention who isn't giving you respect in return, so honor your boundaries and not waste your energy in uncomfortable situations.

I definitely used to be the kind of person who would go through life fully in tunnel vision and wouldn't respond to anyone who ever said anything to me in public. (Wearing headphones without any music playing just so people wouldn't bother me? Been there!) But once I started studying improv, I now look forward to the opportunities of situations like these when they pop up.

Many times I have had very memorable, funny conversations with strangers in the least expected locations- banks, gas stations, even public restrooms- though that's usually a place I try to spend the least amount of time as possible.

Unlike many people, I enjoy interacting with others who are different from me. Usually, our senses put up a red flag and tell us not to interact with someone whom we have no similarities with, and we feel it's dangerous. Lots of outdated ways of thinking and old movies where the villain looks different than the majority have been ingrained into society. But just because someone is different than us doesn't mean they are also dangerous. Again, use your instincts, but some of the best conversations I've had with people who I had nothing in common with. It's fascinating to learn their point of view on life and what goes on in their day-to-day mind.

The first time I visited Japan, I found myself seated at a bar I shouldn't have been at. The handwritten sign in English that read "Locals Only. No Tourists" should have been a giveaway, but here I was, out looking for the unknown in a foreign country. After about twenty minutes of receiving chafed stares from a surly elderly man across the room, he got up and hobbled over to lean on the bar next to me. After saying something in Japanese and a few of the bartenders began to come over to calm him down, I held up my hand to give the international sign for 'wait.' From my pocket, I pulled out my phone and opened a live translation app I downloaded weeks ago in case I needed it for the trip – after all, I don't know Japanese except for how to ask for a refill of water, please. I opened the app and greeted the man in English, translated by the robotic vice. He looks both confused and amazed, yet still annoyed. After a simple nod from me, he responded back into the phone, "Why are you here." It was working!

After a few robotic translations back-and-forth, we learned that he was in town to experience a different culture and that he comes to that bar every night after work, and to "not tell his wife." He, again, like most people, just wanted someone to talk to. Neither one of us expected me to be that person on this particular night, but here we were, using technology to become new friends who would never meet again, as after he bought me a glass of his favorite Shōchū and we talked some more, I had to be on my way. To this day, I imagine that man still sitting in the corner of the smoky bar, just waiting until he finds the next person to talk with.

So be present, listen, and instead of blowing someone off, maybe you can learn more about the world around you without even really meaning to- just be sure you have all the apps downloaded.

Networking

If we put 'dating,' 'job interview,' and 'talking to a random person' in a blender, add some kale, and we'll have networking- and if that word fills you with anxiety, you're not alone. "Networking" is a word I almost dislike as much as "brand," but like that word, it's all about how we look at it.

Networking feels awkward and uncomfortable because we make it so unnatural. When you think of networking, you probably think of some sleazy person in a suit trying to slick-talk you, or sell you something, or force a business card in your hand. But networking doesn't have to be that way. Networking is all about connecting to another person, and as you've learned about in improv, it relies heavily on connecting to other people.

So you have a networking event coming up or you find yourself at a party where you realize you have the opportunity to network. What do you do? Stand in the corner with your drink hoping someone comes over to you? Spoiler: they won't. Or do you step outside of your comfort zone while showing your personality? Spoiler (again): yes, this!

Networking uses a lot of the skills we've already talked about in this chapter because, in a way, it's sort of like a job interview, and it's also sort of like dating, and it's also sort of like a pitch or presentation, and it's also talking to a random person...it's sort of like a lot of things! So using any of the above skills will help here (Matching, Listening, Yes, Anding, etc). But the hardest part of networking might be doing that first thing that Bridges the gap between you standing in the corner and you having a conversation with this other person. So to make that fancy bridge, refer to the chapter about initiations because all of that can be applied here as well.

As long as you are friendly (without being creepy) and use one of those initiation techniques, you'll already be in conversation with this person. It almost doesn't matter what you say or do. You could mention part of the environment that you're in: "Wow, these tablecloths are so cool. Would it be weird to try to have a shirt made from them?" or a word related to the event you are at: "Jupiter. I think that's the next planet this aerospace company is going to travel to.," or start with an emotion "That presentation was so inspiring, don't you think?") - really anything.

Now you may have noticed all of those examples had questions in them, and while we try to stay away from questions in Improv, using them here would be great ice breakers when trying to network with a new person. But like in improv, these questions should not be basic and void of information. If you say, "how's it going?" or "where do you work?" those are boring and put a lot of pressure on the other person to fuel the conversation. But by using a question more related to the present moment (such as the examples above) you can get a conversation going because there's something juicier to respond to. But a word of warning about questions, nobody likes to feel like they're being interviewed in a conversation, so try not to ask question after question after question (after question). After they answer one of your questions, find a way for you to relate to it, make more statements, and find rapport between you two instead of just moving on to another question - basically ignoring their answer they just gave you.

So once you break the ice with your initiation and talk to this person, now is the time to use your personality. Instead of trying to be someone you think you should be as a 'networker,' have fun. Most people don't like networking, so the person you're talking to would rather be doing almost anything other than attending a networking event. Be aware of that fact and have fun when talking to this person. Keep it professional but also have fun. What are things that excite you? What inspires you, and also try to learn what those other people think about those ideas as well? Again, most people love talking about themselves, open up that door and allow them to do most of the talking.

How about an example, huh? Okay fine. One time I was writing for a show, and at the premier, there was a gala that included free food and drinks. Most of the people there were trying to "Hollywood Network" - what I call people being fake and talking about all the things on their resume in hopes that someone can give them a job in the industry. It feels very inauthentic, and most people have a glazed look in their eyes when talking to anybody. To say the least, I felt out of place and didn't really want to play the false communication game. So I changed my perspective and thought, 'I'm just going to have fun.'

At that moment, I saw an executive (I could tell because they had certain color name tags) standing alone, looking sort of lost in the sea of Hollywood fakers. I went up to her, and I said in a playful manner, "Are you okay?" They responded by saying that they were trying to get to the bar to get a glass of water because something they ate was so salty. I said, "Sounds like an adventure. Follow me!" and I beelined through the crowd to the bar like the parting of the Red Sea in that old story as she followed. We got to the bar, and I ordered two waters and we toasted and started talking business. It turns out she was a high level executive at a big network. We exchanged information and a few months later she hired me for a job.

Now I didn't go into that thinking 'I'm going to manipulate the situation to try to get a job offer'. I played it like an improv scene.

I was present in the moment and noticed the strangers 'emotional initiation' of looking lost. And just as you would do in an improv scene, I reacted to it by approaching them and reacting with a verbal line (asking if they're okay) and then Yes Anded their next statement ("Yes, you're trying to get to the bar, and I'm going to get you there!").

Of course, and obviously, this person didn't think they were doing an initiation and had no idea that improv techniques were being used, but they just saw me as someone they connected well with, had a good conversation, and showed my true personality- which then led to the job later on.

So as much as the idea of networking is equivalent to having to go to the dentist to have a deep, painful cavity filled without anesthesia, you could make it an enjoyable experience if you approach it from an Improv Mindset. (and if you get hired for a great job as a result, send me a note and let me know, congrats and how cool!)

Socializing with Quick-Witted Friends

If you're reading this book, or if you're anything like I was before I started doing Improv, then you've probably found yourself in a social situation among friends or family members where everybody is joking around and having fun, and you were having a tough time keeping up with their wittiness. When you finally think of a response to add to the conversation, it's probably way after the time that the subject has already been completed, and you feel even more ridiculous, then when you sat there silently in the first place.

Over the years, I've had a number of students specifically take my classes with the goal of getting better at socializing among their quick-witted friends. And guess what? Improv helped!

Honestly, just like these other sections in this chapter, everything we've been talking about in this entire book can also be used for this improv scenario. What's the best plan of attack when you find yourself in a social situation where everyone is quick-witted you feel like you can't keep up? To Listen and Yes, And.

Instead, most of the time, we try to quickly think of a joke or another topic that we know more about and try to force that into the conversation. But this goes against everything we've learned so far. Instead of thinking of what to say, be in the moment, listen, and simply agree to what someone just said and add something to it. You can keep this as simple as saying 'Yes, And' and then adding your idea or thought. Wow, this is pretty basic stuff for being this far into the book, huh? That's because it is, but like most of these improv scenarios, we make them more difficult than they need to be.

You might be thinking, 'I can't just add *anything* to what someone said? But what if it's not funny enough?' Don't worry we're going to go deep into comedy in the next chapter, which should help you. But the thing to keep in mind when this social roller coaster is in motion, is not to create your own cart but to jump into one that's already moving. So don't try to think of other new, funny things to say, really just add to what someone has already said. The agreement will make you then easily connected to the conversation, and you'll no longer feel like a weird outsider who thinks they should never leave their house again.

Here's a bad example.

> PERSON 1: ...*Like how all animals in the forest get to eat as messy as they want.*
> PERSON 2 (bad): *Um, I always like to use napkins when I eat.*
> (and everyone just stares blankly at you because you changed the subject and weren't playing along).

Now a better example with Agreement.

> PERSON 1: ...*Like how all animals in the forest get to eat as messy as they want.*
> PERSON 2: *Yeah, and they never even use a napkin and get to just walk around with food all over their face, and that's socially acceptable in the animal community!*

See? That second example followed what was already stated and added some new information. It doesn't have to be the funniest thing in the world because it gave the new idea of napkins and the animal community accepting that animals can be messy into the conversation, which can open the door for other people to make jokes on that, and wowy wow, now you're part of the witty banter, yay!

Okay, now I have to give you an example from my life. This will be difficult because there are so many I don't even know what to choose. I used to be someone who would just sit there silently, laughing along and trying to find a way into the conversation. But once I started learning improv, I found these techniques helped me a lot. I pretty much do this all the time now and simply say 'yes' and add something to what somebody else said. So I don't have a specific example because there are millions.

So next time you're in one of these potentially awkward banter situations, don't panic. Just use your improv skills, and it will work out. Then maybe some of your friends will have difficulty keeping up with you.

If you have people in your life who are difficult to communicate with and never let you get a word in, we'll also talk about that in another chapter. I got you.

Customer Service Transactions

This is my number one suggestion as an opportunity to practice your improv skills in everyday life. By transactions, I mean anyone you interact with who works in customer service. This could be a barista, cashier, a server at a restaurant, the person doing an oil change.... the list goes on. We interact with these people all the time, but instead of looking at it as an opportunity to practice our improv and communication, we think of it as an annoying errand that we just want to get over as fast as possible.

I personally feel like everybody should work in customer service at one point in their life just to see things from the other side. People who work in those jobs interact with hundreds of people a week and sometimes even a day. They go through the same motions and spiel that they say hundreds of times, all from a script they had to learn when they went through training to make the customer feel special. Usually, those people are just counting the hours and minutes until they can leave their job and go home and not interact with anybody. So you see, both parties on either side of this interaction don't really want to be there.

This improv scenario is a good opportunity to practice your skills because whatever you do, the other person isn't really going to remember. You were just one random person that they interacted with throughout their busy day. If you interact with them in a way that you normally don't interact with people, they won't even know anything's different. Even if you were to start to talk to them in a strange British accent, how are they to know that's not how you normally sound? Or even if you were to do something crazy... like move your body like a weird alien creature and talk in a weird voice, they might just think you are this way. The worst case scenario is that you will be memorable and they'll tell their co-worker later about this weird customer that they helped. But again they see so many people that after that day they probably won't even remember it, so don't worry about being too embarrassed to show your face in the establishment again. That's why it's a great place to practice any improv skills we've discussed. Try different emotions, physical postures, pretend to be really confident, or be more playful...it's a free practice ground! But it's also a really good place to practice connecting to another person.

In a way, these people are the gatekeepers between you and getting good service. If you neutrally interact with them, or even worse, rudely, then chances are the service they are giving you is going to be subpar what it could be- which is why I never understand why people are rude to servers at restaurants. They're the people bringing you stuff that you put into your body, so wouldn't you want to be extra nice to them, so they don't do anything out of spite to your dish? But that's a completely different topic...

I'm suggesting that instead of acting like just another patron to this customer service employee, why not act like a fellow human? Really connect with this person, even if you're only interacting with them for a few minutes. And I'm talking about beyond just saying, 'how are you?' and they respond, 'good and you?' That's not a connection. That's pre-planned small talk that everybody does all day and doesn't even open things up for you to hear the actual answer to their question. When someone asks 'how are you?' nobody actually wants to hear 'how they are' so let's stop asking that boring question and take these free practice opportunities to connect more than surface level stuff.

If you want to ask how someone is, make it specific. If you noticed that it's busy in the store or restaurant, ask how they're doing with all of the crowds or mention how it must be really stressful for them. Let's use our improv learning by connecting to Emotions. Also, instead of asking empty questions (a big no-no in improv, hello!) assume you know the answer and make a statement or question that way. "You must be so tired of asking every person if they found everything OK, huh?" Start asking a question like that, and you'll start to get actual responses that will break down the barriers of them seeing you just as 'another customer.'

So what would this accomplish? Well, one, you're being nice to somebody who's helping you (yes, even if it's their job). Two, you might even get better service. And three, possibly even a discount or something for free- who doesn't love those things?!

Lots of places have employee discounts for friends and family or promotions going on that they don't advertise in the store- because you're already there, but by acting like a friend to the person working there, they might even give you one of these hidden bargains, as I've gotten many, many times by using these techniques. Make them feel like they're helping out a friend and not just some random person who's making their job a little bit harder, and you may be surprised by the outcome. Obviously this won't happen every time, and don't just be nice to get something in return, but it happens.

With this, I also have many examples from my own life, but one that I'll share right now is when I got into a car accident and had to bring my vehicle to a repair shop for an estimate. Anyone that's been in these situations knows that the mechanic sees this as a great opportunity to make a little bit more money. They can get money from your insurance company and from you if they play their cards right- which they are excellent car-card players. Most people bring their cars into this situation, and they start off from a baseline of already being upset at the mechanic, as if the mechanic was the person who smashed into their car. They assume the mechanic is trying to screw them over and charge them more (which they most likely are), so they are defensive, short, and rude to this person who is just doing their job.

So when I went in, even though I was upset that I had to do this and annoyed that I got into a car accident, and aware that I may be being swindled out of money, I treated this mechanic as if he was one of my best buddies. This is through a friendly tone of voice, open body language, making jokes with him, assuming emotions that they might be feeling, and asking how they're doing based on those, what's going on around us in 'his office', and basically using all of the techniques from improv that we've learned so far in this book - being present, listening, agreement, having fun, etc.

He told me all of the lines that he usually tells customers about 'the problem looks worse than it is,' and 'it's going to cost a lot of money because we have to order parts,' and 'he'll see what he can do,' but by me continuing from this emotion of being friendly, he crunched some numbers and ended up saving me a ton of money on the repairs. So much in fact that I didn't have to pay anything at all, and I don't have a great insurance deductible. Yay improv!

Am I saying to use these techniques to manipulate people? Absolutely not. If you connect more to them as a person, you might get something out of it, but you also make them feel better because you're not being a rude customer and instead making their job a little bit easier. So it's a win-win situation for both sides.

So next time you're in a situation dealing with customer service, which is probably today, use it as an opportunity to practice your improv skills, have fun, and connect to that person as another person because you're both persons...I mean people. You're both people.

Impossible Scenarios

In improv, anything is possible. Improvisers create moments, characters, stories, and entire worlds that never exist right on the spot without anything pre-planned. Creating something out of nothing- it's basically magic, right? Ta-da?

That being the case, we can also use our improv skills to do the impossible in life. There are plenty of situations you can think of right now that seem impossible or others that maybe have never been accomplished before, so it must be an unfeasible task (and I was going to say, 'I'm not talking about obvious things like humans being able to fly' but guess what, we fly every day in planes and there's literally even jetpacks now. So really, anything is possible!)

Just because someone else tells you something is impossible, don't let that stop you. At one point, everything that is done now was something that was never accomplished before. And then, one day, a scientist stole the idea from a lesser-known scientist and got more famous for doing something that had ever existed before. Science! And Stealing!

Sure, when we try something that 'seems impossible' there is a much higher chance of failure, but even if we don't succeed, at the very least, we'll have an exciting story to share possibly for the rest of our life.

To bring all of this back into improv, if we think about it performing improv in front of an audience is basically impossible. Nothing is pre-planned, yet there are just as many successful improv shows as those that fail. And anyone who starts in improv has many failed scenes and shows for a number of months and years until they keep working at it and get that ratio of wins and losses closer to the successful side each time they do it. So even if something seems impossible, you really only fail when you give up. If you keep trying, eventually, you'll figure it out, and then something that seemed impossible is now just something you can do.

This one is probably my favorite improv scenario category, and I could, and maybe should, write an entirely separate book with all the "impossible" adventures I've had through the years. In each instance, I used my skills of Improv to move forward through the situations. But until that separate book is written and released, I'll give you a pretty implausible story right now.

I was in Thailand teaching a class with an improv friend, and later on in the day, using all of the skills mentioned in this chapter, we convinced a tuk-tuk driver to let us drive their vehicle. Now, if you don't know what a tuk-tuk is, look it up, and secondly, they are these driver's livelihood. It's how they make money to feed their family and live. So letting two random people drive it is not a common thing. In fact, afterwards we talked to a local and told them that we drove a tuk-tuk and couldn't believe it either. Anyway, we drove the tuk-tuk, and after heading back to our hotel and feeling amazed by that adventure, I realized that I left my passport in the backseat. Long story short, it was a long story gone.

Well, I was supposed to fly back home in 2 days, but here I was without a passport in a very foreign country. The United States Embassy was closed until later in the week- which wouldn't work because I would miss my flight, and after reaching out to the American ambassador, who told me there was nothing he could do either, I decided to go back to the Embassy and try my improv skills.

So there I was, talking to a security guard behind bulletproof glass in hopes of getting a passport to leave the country in time. Now I feel like most people in the situation would be rude and upset and getting mad at the security guard, who is just doing his job, to let them in and give them a passport, which is not the security guard's job. But since arguing is not a thing, you're supposed to do an improv, and agreement and building off of each other's ideas and listening is, you can probably guess what I did.

After I told him again of my situation (in a friendly tone), I saw them right a note down on a piece of paper. They were writing it in English, so I complimented their handwriting and asked where they learned the language. They told me that one of the relatives lives in the States in an area I knew was getting hit by a tropical storm. Well, one of my own relatives also lived in a similar area, and we both had a connection about worrying about them because of the impending weather barrage. We chit chatted a little bit more, and they stopped, took a moment, and just looked at me. I had no idea what had just happened, but before I could figure it out, they nodded and waved me towards the door. Was I thought what was happening actually happening? It was!

The security guard opened the Embassy on a *day they were closed*, brought me into the office, and we both figured out how to make me a temporary passport so I could leave the country. He absolutely didn't have to do this, and maybe even put his job on the line to do so. But we made a connection, and to him, I wasn't just some rude American; I was another human being just trying to get home.

So I got a replacement passport from an embassy in a different country on a day they were not open to the public. Sounds impossible, but it's true. And it would not have happened if I didn't use my improv skills.

Was I actually relaxed and felt like having a conversation about something other than getting home at that moment? Absolutely not! I was terrified I wouldn't be able to get home and even that they could have taken my perseverance as harassment and called the authorities. But the Improv Mindset improv teaches us to follow the fear. Get outside of your comfort zone and try something you haven't done before. That sounds like doing something impossible, so give it a go, won't you? (...but don't lose your passport, please. It's too stressful!)

The great thing about all these scenarios is that they will actually be easier than any of the improv exercises or scenes you had previously done. In improv, we have to fill in the blanks of who we are, what the situation is, what's happening in said situation, and even where we are. But in all of these real life scenarios, all of those things are already known. We know who we are, where we are, and the situation that we're in. We even know some information about what will be discussed during the scenario ("what would you like to order" for example). The only thing we really don't know is what possible things may come up during that scenario, which is still easier than any of the improv stuff we worked on before because anything that comes up will fit into the scenario we're in- no dealing with zombies or aliens when ordering a coffee...I hope. So if you've been practicing up until now, you've actually been doing something much harder that will make you that much quicker when you find yourself in any of these situations listed in this chapter. Now it's just up to you to make the most of them and practice those skills in real life.

CHAPTER 12

DEALING WITH INEXPERIENCED PEOPLE

S o hopefully, this book has already presented you with new skills so far, and you're ready to really start putting them to use. And if you think you are pretty good at all these improv skills, try dealing with someone you don't know well or someone with a very opposite personality-you'll see there's still more to learn.

After months of practice by yourself and in the real world, it may start to feel like you know what you're doing and there's nothing else for you to learn in improv. What at first was the unknown has now become your comfortable new bubble. But the true sign of a good improviser is someone who can enact these with anybody, regardless if they've ever met before and regardless of the other person's experience with improv techniques, and still be able to have a successful interaction.

If this still sounds easy to you, then try an improv scenario with someone you've never met before. Chances are it's not going to be that good. So how do we get to that next level where we can interact successfully with anybody? It's easier than you think, so here are a few techniques:

Listen

Wow, who would have thought the thing to do here would have been the first and most important rule of Improv!

The less experienced a person is at any of our improv skills (either they haven't learned them or just naturally aren't this personality type), the less of a chance they're going to get into an interaction with you only to support and work together and not just have their own preconceived ideas for how the dynamic will already go.

I was this way after almost six years of performing Improv. It makes sense, though; we don't want to go into the unknown without anything in our back pocket. But the more we practice improv, the more we realize that the best way to be open to anything that happens is to be a black slate and build the situation with the other person.

So knowing that most people aren't trained in improv skills, which means that most people will not go into an interaction without probably having something in their mind already to talk about, is freeing. Let them do most of the talking. The best thing to do is to listen to what they are offering and build off of that. Trying to initiate with our subjects or ideas in hopes that they will let go of theirs is setting us up for a big risk of being shut down.

Therefore, just like we should do in just about every other improv scenario we'll ever be in, just listen. Even if we were the one who started the interaction, we could build off what the other person already has in their head and hopefully work together from there to have a better overall scenario.

Agree

Wait, wait, wait- you're telling me the next thing we need to do is the second rule of improv? This is crazy!

That's right, along with listening, we want to agree to whatever the other person says. Their subject or ideas may seem out of nowhere and completely unrelated to what you said or anything going on around you both, and it might not even be anything that you understand. It doesn't matter, just agree with it and build off of it with them. Listening and Yes, And go together like super glue and fingertips, so we always want to do both together.

As I said, they probably already had an idea when the interaction started, so it's easiest to just get in the boat with them and enjoy going down the river.

Lead

Now, this next tip is something that we normally wouldn't do in an improv scenario, and that is to lead it. Since someone who is newer to improv skills or even bad at them completely, probably already has an idea of what to talk about in their head, it doesn't mean that they know how to execute the overall dynamic better. They may have even started talking out of worry of 'not knowing what to say so I'll say anything' but haven't thought past that of where to take it next. Many times they might just bring up a completely different subject or ask empty questions. Hmm, this sounds a lot like what we used to do before we started to learn all these fancy improv techniques, huh? This is where our true Jedi Master improv skills come into play.

Instead of expressing a great emotion or idea for ourselves, give it to them. For example, normally, we might say, "Yikes, I'm so relieved today because I got all my work done!" but instead, give it to them. We could say, "You look so relieved today, you must have been able to get all of the work done!"

Even if you're wrong, they will correct you, and thus open a new road that you are both now on together and can build the interaction from there. People *love* being right. It feels good to be right. So by assuming (ding-ding-ding, another improv rule!) you will get more information about them and give you both more to talk about. "Oh, you weren't able to get it all done? What happened?"

But giving them an emotion or idea we were going to use on ourselves, opens the floor for them to talk more, and since they started with some random idea, we are supporting them in the frame of mine. It's like, 'oh you want to talk about things, well here's more you can talk about, and I'll just keep Listening and Agreeing because I'm a master at improv now.'

Most of the time, improvisers agree with this and then become stressed, and you can continue the scene from there. However, sometimes they might try to make conflict immediately and disagree with you, saying they did get their homework done and they're not stressed. This is where you lead them by listening and agreeing and, dare I say, asking questions!

Match

We've talked how matching and mirroring is an easy way to connect to someone, so it's even more helpful with someone pushing their ideas. Just keep *Yes, And*ing and matching the ways they are talking and standing. They will feel more comfortable talking to 'someone just like them' and may even open up more and start asking you to talk about yourself. And now we're in a great back-and-forth instead of a one-sided dynamic.

Obviously don't mirror them as if we are mocking them, but do it in a subtle way. If they say something with excitement, respond in the same manner. If they cross their arms, we can subtly do the same. Matching is such a powerful way to make a connection without having to necessarily talk until you find something you both connect on, so it's great to use with someone like we've been discussing in this chapter.

Dead Ends

What if you're interacting with someone who does everything the opposite of what we're saying here. They don't listen, they deny and put down every idea, are more aggressive than supportive, talk over you, and aren't clear on what they want but just like to hear themselves talk (we've all seen this person, and boy, is it frustrating!)

I call these types of people 'Dead-Ends' because no matter what we try to do to be malleable to their personality, nothing gets through and we're are stuck there either listening to them to them ramble on about how 'great they are' or how 'terrible everything is,' and it's basically all about them- a fully one-sided interaction.

Here's the easy solution, buy them a copy of this book, give it to them on their birthday– because you're a nice person, and then tie them to a chair and make them read it cover to cover until they change their ways. Done!

Kidding...mostly. People with these traits usually don't think they're doing anything wrong, and assume everyone else is actually at fault, which is a bad headspace to be in to be able to grow or change as a person. So chances are if you gave them the book, they would make a snarky comment and never open the thing. So if none of the above techniques are working, don't worry- we still have another action plan for you. Walk away.

That's right. It goes against everything we've been learning in improv, but that's what I'm telling you to do. If you tried everything and listening and agreeing and all isn't getting you anyway, you don't have to continue to engage. People like this are bullies, and no part of learning improv is meant to have you be compliant with someone who disrespects your time, ideas, or just you. So you can exit and move on to someone who wants to interact with you.

Why some people act this way towards others stems from unresolved issues from their past, and the only way they know how to engage with people is through aggression. Sometimes they don't even realize they are doing anything wrong because it could be a survival instinct from situations in their past. Other times people can feel threatened by someone else for any number of reasons- some being that we are too different or even that we seem more confident than they are trying to show everyone they are. Whatever the case may be, it's not our job or responsibility to be there for them so they have a human punching bag they can take all their bad habits out on. So leave.

Simply get out there as soon as you're able. Usually sooner the better. Even if they never give you a space to say a polite, "It's been great talking to you, but..." you are allowed to just cut in with any of these exits lines:

> "Hey, I'll be right back."
> "Wait, give me a second."
> "Oh hey, I gotta go."
> "Wait, is that my friend over there?"
> "Thanks, see ya."
> "Talk to you later."
> "And....I'm gone."
> "Oh no, I left my car running!"

Anything you want to get out is helpful- I've used the last two in a number of tough-to-exit situations myself. You don't have to be worried about being rude because this person is being rude to you, and just the fact you had that thought it means you aren't a rude person. Save your energy for someone who actually is interested in engaging with you. You'll be much happier you did, and it will actually be a real place you can use all your new improv skills.

So if you want to get really good at your "Improv Mindset," start having interactions with people you don't know or think aren't that good at communicating- unless it's a Dead End. It will not only make them a little better, but it'll also make you much better.

CHAPTER 13
HOW TO BE PERFECT (AT IMPROV)

This chapter should really be called *How to Get Better at Improv...* since improv is all made up, and so no one can ever be perfect at it, only better

If you haven't tried out your newfound improv skills in the real world yet, now is the time. You're ready. You might not feel as much, and you might still be incredibly nervous, but that's okay, and actually very normal. We can watch as many improv videos as we can find, make our friends and family laugh, or read this book 17 times, and while filling our brain with these powerful techniques is helpful, how well can we apply them counts for anything substantial? These skills are useless until we can make them instinctual. Even if you can carry on a great conversation about creativity and comedy and improvisation, you want to be able to do them without thinking about *how* to do them, and the only way you can get better at improv skills and your "Improv Mindset" is to put it to use and practice. Get out there, fail. Get out there again, and have some good improv scenarios moments and some bad ones. The more you do any new skill, the better at it you'll get. It's as simple as that.

I thought I was good at improv at around year five of practicing it, but then I learned new styles, and it broke all my ol' reliable habits and crutches. At this time, I felt that I was now finally really good- at eight years, I thought I couldn't possibly get better. But it wasn't until the tenth year that I hit these marks. Ten years of doing improv at least once a week, but usually way more, and thinking about it, reading about it, or studying shows for a decade. Once I hit that point, I no longer got nervous before shows but instead felt a sense of calm and could see the entire thing unfolding almost before it did. They say 10,000 to become an expert, but we'll never get close if we don't put in that first hour by getting out in the places where we can fail. Failure leads to growing and learning, which inevitably leads to getting better.

Where to Practice

We already discussed using these skills in the plentiful improv scenarios that exist in our daily life and how you can use bits to practice your improv skills too. But if you want a safer place to work on these techniques, look for improv classes in your town. Improv has spread vastly over the last decade, and chances are there is a group in your town, or at the very least, even some online classes available.[50]

Even if your town has no improv and you don't have access to the intent (because you live off the grid?), you're not out of luck. You can put together your group or club with your friends and practice together at a community center, church, or even in a backyard. When I first started improv, there were only two places doing improv in the entire state I was living in, and each was at least a three-hour drive away. But some of us got a group together and practiced on the weekend for no audience and then eventually felt good enough to talk to some coffee houses that let us perform for a small crowd.

To do this self-taught group idea, you can use resources, such as this book, or any of the other books and videos that exist out there, and run exercises

---

[50] I have some as well, specifically an On-Demand Streaming Improv Course- the first of its kind anywhere. So there's no excuse to learn!
www.Online-Improv.com
Don't try to click this link, you're reading a book. ☺

together. Just remember, everyone is learning, and no one is an expert, so don't get an ego trip and see yourself as some improv guru because you read the most books. Again, we can never be perfect at improv, only get better.

Let's take it another step further and say you really enjoy improv and are excited about the techniques in this book (thank you), but none of your friends are or would be interested in doing this thing. You still have an opportunity to practice. In this book alone, there have been several solo exercises you can do alone with no other human needed. At first, doing improv by yourself will be awkward, and it will be hard to let go of the self-judgment that you are just talking to yourself. But if you really let go and just be in the moment, you will be saying things and responding without thinking ahead or setting yourself up for a funny line. At the end of this chapter, that will be an exercise for you to do solo improv and it's a really good way to keep your skills sharp when there's no one around- as I have done many times.

So as you see, we have no excuse for not practicing our improv, only our unwillingness to do it. Practice makes better; just wait and see how sharp your mind will get.

Goals

If you want to get better at anything, including improv, which I'm assuming you do since that's what this book is about and you are reading this sentence, then you have to set goals and consciously work towards those goals every chance you get. It's that easy. Easy in the sense that we have to just do that, but not easy because it will be some work to get better at improv skills.

It's difficult to get better at something that we're not used to because our minds and our body are already stuck in a comfortable routine. Even if it's a routine we know it's best for us- such as not talking to people or being afraid to give a presentation, we still feel better being in a 'safe place' than stretching out of our comfort zone. But any routine that we're stuck in is something that used to be new for us as well. It just seems easy to us now because we've done it for so long.

Think about the first time you tried to walk... never mind, I don't like that example- who can actually remember that? Instead, let's think about anything new in your life at once. Maybe it was starting a new job, dating someone new, or taking up any new skill you are now proficient at - let's use driving as an example. When we first learned to drive, it seemed over-whelming. We have to have both hands on the wheel, check at least three mirrors consistently, look at the road in front of us, look to the side and back of the car, and use only one foot to control two pedals- all while going upwards of 80 miles an hour in a heavy metal box while being surrounded by other metal boxes zooming around us. Learning to drive is incredibly overwhelming. But we kept doing it, and now we can drive while eating a sandwich, looking at emails, talking to your best friend on speakerphone, and driving with your knee.[51] So while driving that metal box was inti-midating, look at you know. The same goes for any skill, improv included. It's not that some people are born too witty and smart and you won't ever be able to learn improv. You just have to practice.

But if our method of practicing improv is meeting up with a group, or going to a class and doing a bunch of scenes and exercises, then going home and that's it- that's fine. FINE, I say! We just probably won't really get any better at it. But if we want to improve our improv, we have to set goals. This could mean simply setting a goal that we're going to do every practice or class one thing we're not that good at. Maybe a goal is to use one emotion that is most unlike ourselves. Or maybe it's to initiate first,

---

[51] I'm not recommending or suggesting any of this, but you probably can, and maybe, have done this before. Please drive safe.

if we're not good at that. Or maybe it's to attempt a bit with someone we don't know. Whatever we feel like we're not that good at yet, set a tangible goal, be conscious of that goal, and do it the next time we practice.

This doesn't mean we're going to be instantly better at it, but the more we set that goal and put it into action, the faster we'll get better. Then, after attempting that goal, take some time to think about how it went afterwards.[52] We can think about what we should have done instead or what actually worked. Thinking about this after the fact is putting that information into our minds for later use. The more we do, the delay that exists from messing up to thinking about what to do next time will get shorter and shorter until the point that we can enact it instantaneously in the moment and no longer needs to make it a goal, because, guess what, we did it! And onto the next goal...

An easy way to think of some goals is to look at other people we admire or inspire. Notice something they're good at and then attempt to do your own version of it the next chance you get. Let's absorb the powers of the people around us! This also means it's good to challenge ourselves by interacting with people who seem better at thee skills than us. If we want to grow, and feel like nobody else in our circle is challenging our Improv skills enough, that is a great cue to branch out some more. The skills of the new people you start interacting with will be great examples for you to notice unconsciously, and soon, you'll be taking on their traits without even noticing it.

---

[52] a nice rule of thumb is you can't think or talk about the bad things that happened in your improv practice for longer than the event took place. So if you had a ten-minute conversation, you aren't allowed to spend the next two days beating yourself up about something that happened in it. You only get ten minutes to do that and then move on.

Commitment

If you have goals that you regularly practice, then talking about commitment to improv might be unneeded. But it's my book and important, so I'm doing it anyway.

A lot of people think that improv, since it's just 'making stuff up,' doesn't matter much. Why try to actually treat it as more than a skill to get some laughs at a party when we're just making things up. There's nothing to memorize, so who cares! I know you don't think this, but if someone you borrowed this book too does, tell them to please put this book down and never do improv again because they're ruining something that is an actual art form!

One of the greatest jazz albums ever created and still to this day tops off the list of the best overall albums ever is *Kind of Blue* by Miles Davis.[53] Not only is this a great music album, but it utilized a new way of improvising a record that was never done before. That's right, the greatest jazz album of all time was improvised. If those group of musicians just showed up and only cared about getting a few solos in, no one would know this album's name. But instead, they brought their a-game in, were fully committed to the thing they were doing, and worked together as a group, even though they were making it up on the spot.

Well, guess what? The same way jazz uses improv, improv also uses improv (who woulda thought?) So commit to it. No matter how you look at it, improv is an art form. But if you have even spent $1 on learning improv, which you did for this book- unless you stole a .pdf from the internet- then that means you must care about it somewhat. So don't belittle something you are learning and care about, even in the slightest.

---

[53] Also with John Coltrane, Bill Evans, Cannonball Adderley, among others. Jazz powerhouses.

Commitment is needed one hundred percent for anything we do and want to get better at, but even more so with improv. If everything else fails in your improv scenarios, and we have a terrible interaction, with nobody laughing and everyone confused at what we're even talking about, at the very least, we have your commitment to it. It's like what we talked about with the Rule of Three & Infinite. Don't give up on what we're doing because, eventually, it will work, but we have to stay committed to it.

This means that whichever skill we are practicing, go at one hundred percent. If we are doing a bit, don't do it halfway because we aren't sure how it will be perceived. If we look confident while doing something, people just assume we know what we're talking about. So commit, commit! Commit? Yes, commit.

What's The Point?

So what's the point of all of this? What's the point of learning and practicing and wanting to get better at Improv? Most of the time, improv in itself isn't going to pay you any money, or at least not enough to make a living off of. But improv *skills* can lead you to many things that can make money from (public speaking, acting, writing, being the best presenter during meetings...).

If improv itself isn't about building up our ego or becoming a multi-billionaire, then what's the point? Simple. Improvisation is an art form, and like all art forms, it can inspire people. Being a better version of ourselves, using our creativity, and speaking up when we have ideas in our heads can inspire other people to want to do the same. We may have wanted to learn improv to help ourselves, but in the end, demonstrating these newfound skills could end up helping those around you to better themselves too.

Have Fun

Now that all that heavy stuff is out of the way, the most important thing we can do when we're working on your "Improv Mindset" is having fun. Throw caution to the wind and work off of our instincts. At first, it might be awkward, and we may still be stuck in our heads thinking about things that we learned in this book, but at the end of the day, we really have to be in the moment and work off your instincts. Nothing is better than seeing someone in the flow, being confident, witty, charming, and having a good time- especially if it's in a situation we feel less confident in. So here's a little trick- pretend to be confident. Know one will know we're not unless we tell them (either verbally or by our body language or not committing to what we are saying). Talking quietly, asking empty questions, and being unsure of what to say is something nobody wants to deal with. And if we practice these skills daily, then the situations we find ourselves in won't matter much if we fail. Don't wait until that 'big meeting' to start using these skills. Practice, play, experiment and have fun with them in low-stakes situations. That way, when the big one comes, you'll be ready.

EXERCISES: Solo Improv (or Soloprov)

Put everything we've done to use with this exercise.

SOLO IMPROV

Skills Used: *Everything*

HOW TO DO IT

1. Start with a random word and then "role play" an improv scenario using that word as the jumping off point.

PLAY

2. Speak and play both people in the situation, physically jumping back and forth between them, with each responding to the last thing said.

LET GO

3. Ignore the judgmental voice that points out that you're talking to yourself, and really be in the improv moment, and put all of the skills we've learned to use

CHAPTER 14
FEAR

et's talk about the elephant in the room, the four lettered word of fear. Without maybe realizing it, you felt the need to pick this book up and start reading it because of some fear you may have that is stopping you from being the most outgoing, witty, best-version-of-yourself you can be. Above all the lessons and techniques, and theories that improv teaches us, the overall message is how to be more fearless.

In improv, we never want to be ambiguous or middle of the road with our choices or moves in a situation(commit, remember). But even knowing this and practicing these skills, getting out there and doing any improv is a pretty scary thing with a lot of fear that goes into that. But it's the people to keep at improv, whether they have good experiences or ones, that really become the most fearless people.

A lot of nerves might go on when stepping outside your comfort zone, but if we look at the sensations of being nervous, they're the exact same feelings as being excited. When we're nervous, we feel butterflies in our stomach, our hands made shake, our heart beats a little faster, and our body temperature might make us sweat a little bit more.

Now think about the times you were really excited about something. Chances are your body was doing the exact same thing. Maybe nervousness is just really excitement that we label as a negative thing.

I remember an interview with Amy Poehler when she worked at Saturday Night Live and did the Weekend Update segment- a place where she had to play herself, and not have the option of hiding behind a character she was playing. When asked if she gets nervous before sitting at that desk she said, "A friend told me to substitute the word 'excitement' for 'nervous'. That way, you acknowledge the physical feelings without putting a negative spin on things. So sometimes I still get so excited about 'Update' that I want to throw up."

So the next time you're nervous, try to think of it as if you're just excited. Changing what we call it allows our brains not to panic as much. The word nervous comes with a bunch of baggage of what being nervous means, and brings up memories of other times we were nervous, and maybe failed, and before we know it, we end up in a downward spiral and are too nervous about being present at all. But by re-labeling it as excited, our brains associate that with good things and better outcomes, and maybe we'll have less of a chance of wanting to vomit too.

This may be easier said than done, so here are some other things to help us when we are feeling "excited," but your brain is telling us it's a bad thing.

Nervous (...Excited) Before a Situation

Getting up and talking in front of people is one of the top fears that humans have. As a species at the top of the food chain, it's actually pretty ridiculous that the thing we fear the most is being embarrassed. Most people would rather die than be embarrassed.[54]

Every day millions of people from all over the world go out of their way just not to be embarrassed. But here we're learning improv skills used when we find ourselves in a situation with preconceived ideas and attempt not to look like an idiot every time. So it makes sense to be nervous before

---

[54] Our embarrassment probably stems from old survival instincts- if we were embarrassed and made a fool of ourselves, then maybe the tribe would kick us out and we'd have to survive on our own. Luckily that's now how we live in modern society.

stepping into one of these new scenarios. We have no idea what will happen so our fight-or-flight instincts kick in hard, and we feel a rush of adrenaline. That's probably why after successfully completing an unknown scenario that worked well, we feel that high and as if we can conquer anything, because we just basically did an impossible thing, and it didn't turn out so badly. There's no better feeling than overcoming fear.

But that lead up to a situation is tough. Our minds think of all the possible ways things can go (usually badly), and we think of all the reasons we should just turn around and not step outside our comfort zone- it's a lot to manage!

If you're someone who feels this way before you're about to use improv, it's normal. Our improv warm-ups can help to relieve bad anxiety, but here are a few other things we can do:

- Remember.

  Take a moment to yourself and remind yourself of the times you were in an unknown situation and did well. It was possible before, so why not now? That little pep talk can be a great confidence booster.

- Breathe.

  When we get nervous, we have shallower breath and end up giving less oxygen to our brain, so of course our bodies will panic. So take some deep breaths, do some exercises from the Second Circle, and try to relax yourself as much as possible.

- Notice.

  Look around the room and name some things that you see. This will get our minds away from thinking about worst-case scenarios, and get us back to the present moment, where we can more easily be our best selves.

— Move Your Body.

A goal of many of our improv warm-ups is to simply get blood flowing more. Just as nervousness constricts our breathing, it does so to our bodies. They tense up, and we feel rigid, which is not a good place to be to feel free and ready to create. So move around. Even as simple as shaking out our arms and legs, doing a few small jumps, or stretching our neck will make us feel a little better.

— Pee or Poop Scares.

This was my number one anxiety trait, and maybe you feel it, too, even when we don't really have to use the bathroom. I often felt like I had to "let stuff out" multiple times before I did a performance or important meeting out of fear that once I was in the midst of it, I'd have to go so bad that I'd pee my pants. It's never happened- that I know, and the times I wasn't able to use the bathroom beforehand, after the show, I still didn't need to use the bathroom and forgot all about it. But if you're someone who feels better after running to the bathroom, that's okay and there's nothing wrong with that. The alone space might even give you some time to clear your head a little too.

— Stop Trying to Try.

We all want every situation we go into to be the best we've ever done, but the truth is that they won't be. Because any improv situation is collaborative, we can't make anything too specific happen because we can't control what the other person does or says. So, we have to let go of the pressure of trying to make the scenario go exactly as we envision- that will give us more anxiety. Instead, go back to the early rules of improv; just focus on being in the moment, listening, having an emotion (instead of nervous), and building off what the other person says. If we remember to keep it simple, we'll have a higher success rate in better circumstances than if we put a lot of pressure on ourselves to have the best result because this scenario matters more than any others. Relax and remember that no matter what, you'll have other chances to do better if this one fails. But, by thinking this way, chances are they won't (fail I mean).

Nervous (...Excited) During a Situation

To go along with that last point, overthinking the stuff we say during a situation, because it may not be the funniest thing or best thing we can think of in that moment, is also a place you don't want to be in. Trust me, I get it- we don't want to look bad at what we're doing after trying to convince our family, friends, and coworkers that this is our right path. We want them to see all the amazing results you get from being great with people and thinking on the spot and that you know what you're doing in any given circumstance. Well, one, that's too much pressure to put on yourself because things will never be by-the-book-perfect. And two, nowhere in the study and practice of improv does it say putting pressure on yourself will make better results.

The best improvisers are the ones who are confident in their instincts, and perform them fully to the best of their ability... at that moment. That means on a day when we may feel more stressed, or tired, or feeling under the weather might not be as good as the days we're feeling 100%- but that's still the best we can do in that moment- and that's the only place we can go from.

With that, if our instincts are telling us to do something in the moment, whether it's to bring up a different subject, lead more instead of following, or be a little sillier than professional, do It. This book has been about training our "Improv Mindset" instincts, so why would we get an instinctual idea and then let our thinking brain take over and tell us not to do it? Because it could ruin the situation? Because maybe it wouldn't get a laugh or fall flat or be confusing to the other people? WHO CARES!

If it was an instinctual idea you had, and you were using the training you've been working on, and not just doing something for a selfish reason but out of support of the overall interaction, then it was the right thing to do, even if it doesn't make sense to you.

We will never get better at improv if we squash our own instinctual ideas and then only talk about them afterwards to try to get approval from people when the scenario was already done. Such as, after a situation saying to a friend:

PERSON 1: *I was going to say this funny thing, but I didn't...*
PERSON 2: *Oh, that would have been good, you should have!*
PERSON : *Okay, I will next time.*

No, you won't. Because next time you'll still be second guessing your instincts. If you didn't do something out of worry, sure, maybe it would have ruined the entire situation and made you look like an idiot, or maybe it was a good idea, and it will be the best part of the night. You don't know. The best that happens is that it's amazing, and the worst that happens is it wasn't. Oh well.

A great thing about improv is no matter how bad it goes, we will never ever see that moment again- it exited only for that time. But the opposite is true because no matter how great something went, we'll never see it again. But the most important thing is did you learn from it.

If you made a move and it flopped hard, you can almost guarantee you will never make that mistake again. And, wow, you've made ten mistakes you've learned from? Well, that makes you ten times stronger than someone who hasn't. Look at you!

We learn improv because we want to get outside our comfort zone, enjoy the freedom to do, and be whomever you want to be at that moment. So let's stop using our time of improvising to second-guess ourselves. We've already done that enough for one lifetime, don't you think?

After the Situation

You did it! You faced your fears and used your "Improv Mindset" to do your best during an unknown situation. How did you feel it went?

It's easy to say we had a good scenario if the other people laughed, shook our hand at the end of the conversation, or said that they'll be in touch, but that doesn't necessarily mean we had a good scenario. To truly get better, we have to also ask ourselves how were the moves we did during the situation.

Did you follow the techniques in this book; Listen, Agreement, use Emotions, really connect to the other people, or just make random jokes that you thought of beforehand? Sometimes our audience just isn't feeling what we're doing, but you can be doing great moves anyways. True, the best case is when both sides are aligned, but sometimes it just doesn't happen. So maybe there were some things you could have done better or maybe some techniques you knocked out of the park, homerun-that's great. It really doesn't matter what happened as long as we can look at it and think about what to improve on next time, and there will always be a next time

Or maybe we know it was horribly bad, because the other side told us to our face that it was bad. It stings, but again, so what. Take the lessons from it, learn, and try to have a better situation next time.

It's easy to beat ourselves up for days, even months, after something goes wrong, so a good rule is that you're not allowed to dwell on a bad scenario for any longer than that it took place. So if you had a five-minute conversation that was the most embarrassing five minutes of your life, you only get five minutes to feel terrible about it, then let it go.

Focus on the good. There will always be not-as-good situations because WE ARE MAKING EVERYTHING UP ON THE SPOT, but don't hold on to them. Just as with life...let go of that time someone hurt us; it's not going to fix things or make us feel any better holding onto it.

No matter how much we feel like we're a superhero or a rock star after a good improv scenario, all outgoing people are still just ordinary people. People with improv skills just happen to be ordinary people trying to do extraordinary things extemporaneously. The greatest feeling is having someone compliment you on what you just made up on the spot. Asking, "How did you think of that?" or, "You were so funny!" or, "Wow, you are great at interacting with strangers." Those come and go. Sometimes we win, and sometimes we won't. But remember, even when you have down days in the valley, the highs of the mountain peaks are just around the corner.

Be Like the Scoops

Be like the scoops. With potato chips, we prefer the ones that are twisted and rolled- like scoops. But those of the mistake ones! Chips were made to be flat and thin, but the ones that accidentally curl are the ones we like the most. They even make a brand that are all 'mistake ones' called Scoops that we buy specifically because they're different.

We're all born unique and grow up having our own tastes in everything from food, music, and even colors. But we then spend our lives trying to be like everyone else and to fit in. It's not anyone's fault, that's just how our society works.

The people who raised us didn't know any better because of the people who raised them, so all we know how to do is to socially train our children to try to fit into society as we ourselves learned. A kid dressing up like an animal and jumping on furniture has to be corrected, so they don't become a 'wild adult' who does that and thus isn't able to get a job and then ends up living on the street, and it's all the parents' fault for being a bad parent, oh no!

But by squashing these creative desires, we aren't taught that there are still appropriate times to use them. So instead, we all become mindless lemmings following each other based on what someone told us we should and shouldn't do, while no one is being creative or individually thinking for themselves.

We as humans like to find ourselves in groups of people who are similar to us, which comes from insecurities. Our unconscious thought is, 'If we surround ourselves with other insecure people, we feel a little stronger.' It's the idea behind the saying 'misery loves company' - people who complain like being around other people who support their complaints because they feel less terrible and there's no pressure to change. A safe but unhelpful comfort zone.

We feel safe here, but it will never allow us to grow to become better people and thus have better lives. Step outside that group and be that strong person for yourself. We all did that when we were younger- playing for hours at a time alone in our rooms. You never needed anybody else. You never needed someone's permission to be yourself, and guess what? You can do that now as an adult too. Be that strong independent person on your own. You don't need to hide behind a group to keep playing small and being like the herd.

The world does not need more people fitting in. The world needs creative individuals to think outside the box and come up with new ideas. That's what we all want! Nobody wants to see the same movie remade 16 times. We want to see new ideas and something that surprises and inspires us. The best inventions that we have in our world came from someone who thought outside the box. They got creative and innovative, and they didn't let other people's judgments stop them.

We live in a time now where we are more connected than ever. We can open up an app on our phones (on our telephones!) and see what someone else who lives on the other side of the globe thinks about something. Their opinions affect us, and we can start thinking the same way. We have no idea who these people are, what culture they live in, or what their upbringing was. Yet we are so quick to judge harshly or agree immensely with these strangers- who usually portray a version of themselves that is not even who they really are in real life.

As such, over the last few years, the world's population has had to face and live through trauma that most of us don't even recognize. We're being told conflicting ideas about how to live, look, and be all from videos on a screen. And as anyone who has done any therapy knows, trauma that isn't worked through can affect other areas of your life. It can make us start acting in ways we normally wouldn't act and take things out on people who we don't even know. All of this stops us from being present in the moment and reacting to what's in front of us now instead of reacting to past experiences, or worse, how someone told us to react.

What does this have to do with a book about improv? Well, I think you know the answer. Improv skills are life skills. It teaches us not to do what other people think we should do, but to step outside of our box and be our most creative and unique selves.

Now I'm definitely not saying to go out and be offensive, hurt people, or start your own society 'off the grid,' but use the creativity that you had as a kid only now as an adult in this world- FOR the world. We all need more of that joy and creativity. That's what we all want to experience. There's already enough fear going around, so be someone less afraid. Follow those gut instincts and be creative. Be you!

We live in a non-participation society where we normally watch people do things we wish we could. We watch people on TV or social media doing things that we wish we could do. Well, I'm saying do those things. Don't live by society's rules of just fitting in and watching life from afar. We used to be a species that would participate, dance, and try to better those around us. So I'm asking you now to participate in your own life.

> "*Nothing great* was *ever achieved without* enthusiasm"
> ~ Ralph Waldo Emerson

You are reading this book because you decided to take some steps to grow and become a better version of yourself than you used to be. That's big work, so kudos to you for taking those steps!

It's not an easy task because anyone who tries to step outside the box of normal society gets judged. It's just how humans are. We judge others for things we're afraid to do ourselves. We don't want other people succeeding because it will make us feel we're not doing enough.

But never let these judgments stop you. When you're judged, that just means you're doing something right. Otherwise, you would have never gotten that reaction out of someone.

Keep your dreams and goals alive. Believe you can do them. Imagine you can do them, and you will do them! It doesn't matter if someone else believes in you or not. Yes, it feels better to be supported by those around you, but sometimes it just doesn't work out that way.[55] But even if that were so, others' belief in you means nothing if you don't fully believe in yourself. You had these dreams and goals for a reason, so believe in them.

An easy first step is to use these improv skills to remove some of our fears about life. You'll find out that other side isn't actually scary but way more fun. So be different than you're supposed to be because that's what we all like anyway. Be like the scoops.

Failure is Part of the Process

No one ever was great or even good at something when they first attempted it. It takes years of trying and failing to get better and learn anything-improv included. If you know that along your path, failures only mean you are trying and at the very worst, you will have quite the adventure and learned a lot while becoming a stronger person in the process. Know that it is okay to fail. Failing is not a failure! Society might say that failing is bad, but again, that's only so people don't try anything and won't feel bad

---

[55] Author Jim Rohn once said we're the average of the five closest people in our lives. So try to surround yourself with people who align with the life you want.

about themselves when they fail (because it's their first time trying something new, so they probably will). It's the people who have tried many times and then succeeded that we all look up to for a reason. So again, fail as much as possible because that only means you are on your way to succeeding!

Bumps in the Road

As humans, we prefer things that break the normal pattern of life. For instance, in music, most people's favorite moments in a song is when something changes- the syncopation. Musicians work so hard to create a catchy or original melody, rhythm, or chorus, but our favorite part is when the music changes the pattern they set up such as when the music stops for a moment before coming back or when a 'beat drops,' something that is different from the rest of the song. That's our favorite part. We like the things that break the pattern.

We like vacations, or celebrating holidays and birthdays- we like things that are different from normal everyday experiences. But how interesting that we then shy away from new experiences every day and want things to go along our pre-conceived and planned ideas, as if we want them to be the same normal boring life. I know I can be guilty of this as well.

I love traveling. But any time it's leading up to packing my bags and heading to a new place, I think about cancelling the trip and say I don't feel like going away. Yet every time I'm at the new destination, I love it and want to spend even longer there than planned. Our routines are comfortable, but that doesn't mean we really enjoy them.

Adventure in life comes from when things are different and those moments that change the everyday pattern in our routine. Those are the best moments in life, so seek out that adventure, have fun, and find the humor and play in everything because, really, that's what we enjoy.

My True Reason for Teaching

Okay, time for me to come clean with a little truth about why I teach Improv. Yes, it's to help people get better at being funnier and thinking quicker, and watching a good long form improv show that is entertaining and memorable is pure magic for sure. But really, I started teaching because I saw people who went through the programs at other schools but still would get on stage and then be nervous and have no fun at all. Being able to talk about these improv ideas is one thing, but getting out there and doing it, while radiating with fun, is more important.

For me, improv really brought me out of my shell and allowed me to be more of the free-spirited and creative person I was when I was a kid- before societal fears suppressed my true self. So secretly, when I teach improv, it also aims to bring that out in other people. Learning improv liberates you from the shell that life has put us in. The rules and techniques performers learn on stage translate incredibly well to our human lives. It makes people more accepting of other people, better communicators and listeners, and more caring people. And if more people can be like that in the world, then that's the kind of place anyone would want to live in.

So what really resonates with me as a teacher of improv is seeing people being their best, brave, confident selves. That's why I teach, and that's what I hope you get from reading this book.

The Month That Changed Everything

For me, the event that finally pushed me over the edge from being my past nervous self to my self now, who has more fun in life and looks forward to different experiences happened a few years ago. Over just one month, three separate people who were close to me unexpectedly died.

Everyone loses loved ones in their life, and maybe most probably handle it better than me, but this really hit me hard. Here were three people in my life: joyful, positive people who never took advantage of anyone else- so by all means, good people, taken out of this world, and I would never physically interact with them again. Just like that, gone. Bye.

Now I could have ignored this, or just have been sad for a while and then moved on with my life, but I couldn't. Not this time. Death is a permanent thing; as much as we ignore it and don't talk about it, it doesn't make it go away. As humans, we are well aware of the many diseases and causes of death that kill people every day, but the thing that nobody talks about is that we all have an illness- an illness called Death. No matter what you do in your life, whether you take care of yourself or you don't, all of us will die. We are all on a ticking clock.

Not to be morbid, but you can die ten minutes from reading this by someone driving a car and not paying attention, or from thousands of other freak accidents. Now I hope that your time will be the best case scenario where you are very old, laying in a comfy bed, surrounded by all of your loved ones, but much like an improv scenario, we can't *know* it will happen like that.

Either way, when it's our time to finally go, and we are taking our last few breaths, do you think you'll be there saying, "I'm so grateful I never took any risks in life and played it safe like everyone else. I'm so glad I ignored my instinctual feelings on things that I wanted to do and places I wanted to go during my life. And OH WOW, I'M HAPPY I never went outside of my comfort zone and used my creative imagination in public because there could have been a small chance that I would feel embarrassed!" I highly doubt it.

There are plenty of articles interviewing dying people on their biggest regrets, and while most of them say things like, 'I wish I didn't work as much,' or, 'I wish I traveled more.' none of them ever say that they wish they didn't risk having more fun.

So at the very most, live your life the way you want, because if you live from the advice of your family, friends, and neighbors, you will never be truly happy. And at the very least, doesn't it seem a little ridiculous now to be too afraid to do something in an improv scenario? Like what's the worst that could happen? We're not going to die from feeling embarrassed!

In fact, if you think back to the biggest stresses you had even a year ago, they probably don't seem that big a deal right now. When you think back on them, it only takes up a moment in your mind. But when you're in the middle, it seemed like the end of the world. When we put events that we give so much energy and put so much pressure on into perspective, in the long term of our life, they really shouldn't matter as much as if you enjoyed yourself.

Improv is all about being in the moment. And all we have every day are moments that make our up precious time because once a moment is here, it's gone. This moment right NOW? Gone. This moment, HERE. Over. This one, too, it's done. No going back. Every moment is fleeting time, so make the most of it before you run out because you will. We all do. Because if we can make the most of each moment of our lives, every chance we get, then we're going to have a fantastic life.

Final Thoughts

We all have three choices for tomorrow. We can either be worse, be better, or be the same as today. At the very worst, you want to be the same. Life gives us endless opportunities to grow and be more of the people we want to be, but it's up to us to choose. It takes work going against the grain every day, but little at time, taking small steps. Soon, we'll look back and feel proud of where we are.

Fear is the thing that stops us. But can be stronger than the fear in our heads. We judge ourselves more than anyone else ever will. And if that's true for us, it's true for everyone- which means other people are too busy judging themselves to ever judge you.

Step outside the box everyone else is hiding in and lead your own life. Don't just follow what everyone else is doing so you don't get judged by them. Who cares? Don't be a sheep, be someone who runs ahead of the herd. When you were a kid, you didn't want to sit behind a desk and be bored all day, just counting the time until you could have a few hours of fun during the weekend. You wanted to create; you wanted to be on adventures, so do that now! We really don't need more people fitting in, so stop trying so damn hard to be like everybody else. Be the creative person I know you can be. Live in the moment, listen, respond to what's around you, Yes, And, and have fun in life. Give yourself the permission to have the most fun you've ever had in your life, because, as far as we know, this is all we get. Plus, you may even inspire others around you to do the same.

So when the unknown comes your way, don't run from it, but remember- it's all the game. You now have some techniques to play the game better than before, and you can use these to make you a better person. Use your superpowers! You can think outside of the box a little bit more, play just a little bit more, and hopefully be yourself even more. So play the game, have fun, and chase down the fear. Never let fear stop you from doing something outside your comfort zone or being more fully you. With this mindset, you can do great things, and we need people like that in the world.

I know you can do it.

FINAL EXERCISE: Goals (Part 2)

Remember when I had you make a list of goals at the beginning of the book and told you to put them aside? Well, get them out, because we're going back to them now!

GOALS: PART 2

How to Do It:

1 Go back to the list of GOALS we made at the start of this book

2 Choose one, and really try to go after it using the skills you learned. Do a little bit everyday, but don't stop until you reach the end!

3 Once complete - CONGRATS!! Cross it off the list and go for another.

CHAPTER 15

MY STORY

was creative as a kid, as most of us are, but after enough other people told me to stop being me, I shut down and became synonymous with a piece of furniture.

I'd ride the bus to school, and every day, I hoped for no one to ever look at me or speak to me. I just wanted to sit quietly and make doodles in my notebook. I couldn't even talk that much among friends. When we had to give presentations in a class, I would either go first, to just get the nightmare over with, or would go last- in hopes that the teacher would forget about me. They never did, and I'd stand up there gripping my piece of paper with both hands as if it was all I had in the world. I would shake uncontrollably, sweat like a dolphin,[56] and could hardly breathe whatsoever. You'd think I'd never want to get up and perform for an audience, but the creative bug was still inside me for whatever reason.

In late high school, I signed up to be an anchor for the on-camera morning news club, and appeared on camera in front of the entire school- yet still shaking and out of breath. I guess I liked it enough to keep coming back because I did it for two years, and it was the place where my shell started to slightly open by doing (what I now know as Bits) here and there when on camera- little things like saying the cafeteria menu in a French accent, or pretending I fell asleep when the camera cut to me. I was still incredibly

---

[56] Do Dolphins sweat? During those presentations I would sweat so much I'd be as damp as a dolphin...because they live in water.

nervous, but it became fun to play around- and get in trouble with the teacher who was in charge for not being 'professional enough.'

When it came time to fill out our college applications, all my teachers urged me to continue on my path of the visual arts, something I've done for as long as I can remember. But for whatever reason, I chose Theatre.

I was accepted into a University Conservatory Theatre program and studied Script Analysis, Methods of Acting, and Scene Study along with my peers, who were all stage brats their entire life. At this time, I still had never been in a play, and all these theatre classes were actually fairly boring to me- but I thought that's what I had to do to be an actor and get to that free feeling of playing ever again. So I put my head down and continued the studies that were uninspiring to me.

But then, luckily, a series of events that looked like failures at the time, that I won't go into here,[57] led me to an "Acting For Non-Majors" class that had an entire focus entirely on Long Form Improvisation. The teacher, and soon-to-be friend, just completed the Summer Intensive Program at the Improv Olympic (iO as it's legally known) and taught us Chicago-Style Improvisation page-by-page from his notes. Here was a place to play and fail and have fun, all with people that supported each other along the way. I fell in love with it almost immediately.

The first few weeks (ehem...months), every scene I would do would result in me either playing air guitar or falling on the ground, scraping my elbows and knees. I had improv class Every other day, four times a week. The off days were used to tend to 'floor wounds', while the other days, I'd be right back to bloody limbs again. Basically, I had no f'n clue what I was doing,

---

[57] I auditioned for the school's "Improv Club" multiple times and never would be accepted, but was told I could try to audit an improv-based Non-Majors Acting Class. See, I didn't get into the story 'up there,' but I did here.

in improv or performing for that matter. Our final exam was a long form improv show at a nearby coffee house, and more than 20 years of improv later, I'm still doing it.

The point of me sharing all of these details was to demonstrate that I started from a place of fear and zero knowledge. I hurt myself while learning this skill (which is not what anyone should be doing), but I slowly learned. In all my years of teaching, I am happy to report that not one of my students have ever left a class with blood on them. Improv is the only art-form where you can never become perfect- but you can walk away uninjured.

Once I got hooked on improv, I read every book available on the subject, some good and some not-so good (bad). I watched videos online, when there weren't really any,[58] listened to podcasts, and went to see the only improv in my town, which was short form and not what I was learning or really interested in at the time.

I eventually studied from the country's biggest schools and some of the greatest teachers on the subject. It took me years, lots of trying and failing, trying and succeeding, and way too much money.

Meanwhile, I saw people around me spend the same amount of time and money but still fail. They were going through some of the improv school "factories" and not really learning or being freed. They never had the benefit of what I had when starting out- that of being in a small, focused group, and working on the art form from that intense level. So I started teaching.

To date, I've now taught all around the world in over ten countries, worked with some of the biggest companies and film studios around to help them become more creative thinkers, performed Off-Broadway, wrote with some of my comedy heroes, and have helped thousands of students who have

---

[58] Fun fact: the group that grew out of that first coffee house show, also became very first long form improv video ever posted to YouTube. We're internet famous! (not really)

taken my classes become more confident, funnier, and best of all, more of the people they really wanted to be but were being held back from the outside world.

I started this book years ago and would revisit it off-and-on for just short of a decade. Every time I'd sit down to continue it, things had changed. I grew as a person, my view of life and creativity had grown, and improv itself can never be stagnant. As an art that exists only in the moment, it's ever-evolving. At one point, we can think that we know the best and most effective way to approach it, but then the more you do it, you find even better techniques and ideas that work. I've found that the more I would grow as a performer and comedy writer, the more those skills would apply to life.

My goal with this book is that you can grow a little bit too. Improv really did change my life, and if these words I'm writing on this digital paper can affect or inspire you even in the slightest- to look at your life and the world from a new perspective, to show you that change, with enough practice and focus, is possible- then I have done my part. The rest if now up to you. But luckily, the worldwide community of improv is ever-growing, so remember, you are never really alone in the journey.

EXERCISES & WARM-UPS

ere are some bonus exercises and warm-ups that weren't listed earlier in the book. Some of these you can do on your own, and some are also instructed to do with a group, so gather your friends or co-workers and try some out!

Patterns (Group)

Skills Used:

* Quick-Thinking
* Listening
* Focus

This warm-up works on focusing, listening, and staying in the present moment.

How to Play:

1) Everybody in a circle will raise one hand.
2) One person, usually the teacher or coach, chooses the category (for example: Animals) and one at a time, someone points to somebody else in the circle with their raised hand and says an animal (Dog, Mouse, Turtle, Manatee, Lion, Eagle, etc.).
3) Then that person points to somebody else in the circle whose hand is up and says a *different* animal (you cannot repeat any that have been already stated).

4) This continues until everyone has gone, and it circles back to the first person.

5) Then continue this same pattern, pointing to the same person you just did and saying the same thing you just did, for a number of times until everybody gets used to it. This will be Pattern Number One and will be paused for a moment.

6) Now start a completely fresh one with a new category (for example: Vegetables) with the first person pointing to somebody different than before in the circle.

7) This continues around as before, but now with Vegetables, everyone hopefully pointing to a different person than the first pattern.

It's important to point to someone different if you can to help things out later in the warm-up. If it works out where you're pointing to the same person because you don't have a choice, that's okay too.

8) After doing this pattern a few times by itself and until everyone gets used to it, Pattern Number Two will be paused as well.

9) Now, we're going to layer them on top of each other (as we do in Pass the Gesture/Phrase). The first person can start Pattern Number One again and then toss Pattern Number Two into the mix after a few words.

10) So now we have two Patterns, just as we did when they were separate, but now they are being done over each other. We're still pointing to the same person you did for the first and second rounds. Don't change anything you did.

Sometimes you might have both Patterns sent to you at the same time, and in that case, you have to send them one after the other. But this game isn't about waiting until you have two things. You should send your word as soon as you get it and then eagerly await until you get the next one.

11) Once everyone gets the hang of this, we put those two Patterns to the side, and we create a new one with a new category (for example: Musicians or Bands), and the same thing happens as before with this new pattern, pointing to a new person, and repeating a few times until everyone feels comfortable.

12) Now you try to layer all three on top of each other without dropping any and while staying in the same rhythm as the Patterns were in when sent by themselves.

This warm-up's **goal** is really about focusing because as soon as you zone-out and don't pay attention, one of those words is dropped, and the Pattern dies. So everybody has to do their part to be ready to send it to the next person.

Tips:

– it's everyone's job to ensure the person they send it to receives that word. You can't just point to someone, shout a word, and move on- especially when we get to three rounds going at the same time because it's going to be noisy. Make eye contact with them and be sure they receive the word, so the pattern doesn't disappear into the improv ether where forgotten names and invisible furniture go.

– If, and when, something gets dropped, instead of someone shouting out, "Hey, where'd the vegetables go?" which will only stop the game entirely, the first person to send out that specific pattern should notice it was lost and restart it into the mix.

– It also helps to keep in mind specifically who sent you what word and who you're sending to for each Pattern. It's not so much being aware of everyone else in the group except the people you interact with.

This warm-up might seem impossible, especially the first few times you try it, but once everyone focuses, it's amazing when you get to those three overlapping rounds and get in the zone of listening...there's that number one rule of improv again!

187 Walk into a Bar (Solo or Group)

Skills Used:

* Quick-Thinking
* Puns

This game is known by many different numbered titles, but we'll stick with this one. 187 is a fun short form improv game where you pretend to be a stand-up comic (without having to hit that grueling open mic circuit).

How to Do It:

1) Get a list of objects (either make your own or a random list from a website).
2) Then, use the following setup to start telling a joke that ends with a pun-filled punchline.
   "187 [nouns] walk into a bar. The bartender says, 'sorry, we're all full' and the [nouns] reply [with a pun]."

Example:

PERSON ONE: *187 cars walk into a bar. The bartender says, 'Sorry, we're all full' and the cars reply, 'Well we'll just roll on out of here then. Or: ...we don't care, we're going to park our butts down.*

Or: ...*we just need a quick fill-up*
Or: *BEEP BEEP, WE'RE THIRSTY!*

Do a few rounds with each object before you move on to a new one. The **goal** with this is quick-thinking and connecting different objects to different things related to them. In improv, someone will say something, and your brain connects the multiple ideas that you can use throughout the scene. The same muscle is worked here.

Tips:

- Try to get a bunch of things in your head related to whatever the object is. For example, if it was a *car,* you might think of: *tires, gasoline, oil, seatbelts, windshield, a steering wheel,* or you can think about what cars do (*drive, cruise, roll, park*), and those can be something related to what your punny punchline is.
- Start saying the setup of the joke out loud with no punchline in mind and see if you can come up with one by the time you get to the ending. Don't want to strengthen overthinking, but quick thinking. Try it. You may surprise yourself.
- Not every joke has to be hilarious. The point here is building ideas off of a subject, so don't worry about saying some that go flat. *(car pun INTENDED!)*

Thunderdome (Solo or Group)

Skills Used:

- * Listening
- * Quick-Thinking
- * Connecting Ideas

Two people enter, and only one survives. This is Thunderdome!

In all of the classes where I've ever done this warm-up, whether it be for executives at movie studios or for people in a small village in Thailand, and everybody in between, they all seem to very much enjoy Thunderdome.

How to Play:

1) Start by circling up (yep, again)...and two people enter the circle.
2) They are given a category, such as *colors*, or *bands*, or *modes of transportation*, or *types of clothing* - any category with many things in it (so *people named Walt Disney* wouldn't be a very good category).
3) Each Person in the center will go back and forth naming things in that category as fast as possible.
4) They aren't allowed to repeat any that have already been said, say things that don't belong in that category, and can't take too long to answer. If they do, everybody on the outside of the circle are the Thunderdome Judges and will be looking for these mistakes. If one of them happens, a judge shouts "Thunderdome!" and the person who messed up is out of the circle.
5) Another challenger is the person who messed up, and the game continues with the objective being to stay in the middle as long as possible.

This game has similar **goals** to Word Association and works on how quickly you can think of different things when the pressures are on (such as being in the middle of the Thunderdome). When you're in an improv scenario (such as a conversation) and someone mentions a subject or object, your mind should be able to connect to other related things and add them to the dialogue.

Tips:

- To add some dramatic tension and pressure to the game, these judges on the outside of the circle will also clap the outer part of their legs in unison
- If you are in the middle of the circle, you cannot call Thunderdome on the other person or yourself. So, if the category is *colors* and you accidentally say pizza. Maybe no one will catch it and just keep going.
- A lot of times when this game gets started, some people are too nervous to call Thunderdome, so whomever the leader of the group is can start doing it at first. Eventually, the group will get the hang of it, but really urge everyone else to notice when people make a mistake and call out "Thunderdome!"
- After everyone has gone at least once. I usually like to announce that 'there will be five more final rounds' to see who the final champion will be. This is also a good opportunity to have people go again or someone who did a really good job to challenge the current champion and try to win the game.

Thunderdome- always fun to have some friendly quick-thinking competition, so enjoy.

Solo Version:

Play this game alone by making a list of subjects on pieces of paper and drawing them from a hat (or to use less paper, use a random subject generator website) and then start naming as many objects in that category as possible until you Thunderdome yourself for messing up.

Ba Da Da Da /Electric Company (Group)

Skills Used:

* Listening
* Quick-Thinking

This warm-up commonly has two different names. Electric Company came from the very old segment on Sesame Street where two profiles of faces would each say a part of a word and then combined those words create a new work. This was done *slightly* more recently on an episode of Family Guy as well.

Bad Da Da Da comes from the sound that is made while playing this game. Simple enough.

How to Play:

1) Everybody circle up (I'm never not going to say it)! The group will begin by snapping their fingers in unison at a slow rhythm.
2) One Person will say the first part of a word.
3) Immediately after, and on the very next *snap*, the person to their left will complete it with the second half of what the word might be.
4) Then the full group repeats the whole word and says, "Ba-Da-Da-Da!"
5) That second person then begins a new half-word, and the game continues.

Makes sense? Should we move onto the new warm-up? No? Good, that's why there is this sample version:

Example:

PERSON 1: *Chip-*
PERSON 2: *-munk*

EVERYONE: *Chipmunk. Ba-Da-Da-Da!*
PERSON 2: *Tie-*
PERSON 3: *-dye*
EVERYONE: *Tie-dye. Ba-Da-Da-Da!*
PERSON 3: *Junk-*
PERSON 4: *-mail*
EVERYONE: *Junkmail. Ba-Da-Da-Da!*

This continues around and around the circle, hopefully getting a bit faster as it goes on.

Again, the second part of that word has to be said *immediately* on the next snap. We don't want someone to say the first half of the word, and then there are all these snaps with nothing said while they think of the next part of the word. We're working on quick thinking in improv, so you just have to respond as quickly as possible.

Now sometimes you might say a second half of the word that doesn't really make sense, but that's okay...for now. There's no wrong answer except for no answer. You want to have the full word make sense, but I prefer speed to overthinking until everyone gets used to how to play.

The **goal** of this warm-up is listening in the moment and responding fast. You have no time to think ahead because you have no idea what word the person next to you is going to set up for you to finish. So you have to stay focused, listen, and respond in the moment. I would rather see someone complete the word and then question why that came out of their mouth instead of taking time trying to think of a better answer.

Also, the first part of each word doesn't have to be a word that can stand on its own (for example, "chip" or "tie") but can also literally be the first *parts* of words that have multiple syllables. For example: "Yester...." "...Day" or "Coff...." "...ee."

Tips:

- I've said for years that if I ever wrote an improv book, I would add a trick I found related to this game, so I'm going to do it here, now to be forever frozen in time and used by anyone who reads this.

For almost every second-half of a word, you can say the word "house," and it would make sense. Boathouse, poolhouse, doghouse, even chiphouse and junkhouse kind of make sense. Now that I said that, I don't want you to just rely on the crutch of always saying *house* because that's cheating, and if you're cheating at an improv warm-up you're really not getting the purpose of what the game is. But just throwing it out there because it's funny how almost anything could be a house. End of paragraph-house? Nope.

Until the World Ends (Solo or Group)

Skills Used:

* Storytelling
* Building Ideas

This warm-up game focuses on heightening situations, aka making things more ridiculous than they were before, which is a great thing to do if you want to add more humor to situations, since most comedy is exaggerated, ridiculous situations happening in unexpected places. But more on that later, right now we're still talking about warm-ups; calm down Keith.

This is similar to the *Yes, And* exercise, except it works on heightening a story instead of just going through one, and is usually a little bit darker sense of humor.

How to Play:

1) Dare I say... with everybody in a circle, someone starts with a boring regular 'ol phrase.
2) The next person repeats or paraphrases that statement and then says what happened as a result of that first statement, making things in the story slightly worse than they were before.
3) The next person repeats that previous statement, making the situation worse with the next statement.
4) This continues until it leads to the destruction of planet Earth.

Now you could make large jumps in this game where someone might say something like, "I got in a car crash" and the next person could say, "and then the world ended!" sure. But it's much, much better, and the goal should be, to organically lead up to the end of the world where everyone in the circle is in agreement that the next thing that happens will be the end of the world.

Example:

PERSON 1: *I can't find my shoes.*

PERSON 2: *I can't find my shoes, and I'm going to be late to work.*

PERSON 3: *I'm going to be late for work, and I'm probably going to get fired.*

PERSON 4: *I'm going to get fired, and I'm not going to have money to pay my rent.*

PERSON 5: *I'm not going to have money for rent, and I'm going to have to live on the street.*

PERSON 6: *I'm going to have to live on the street and pickpocket people for food money.*

PERSON 7: *I'm going to pickpocket people until I get stabbed by someone.*

PERSON 8: *I get stabbed by someone, and the rusty knife gives me a weird infection.*

PERSON 9: *Since I don't have money or a job for health insurance, I have to go to a shady doctor to have the infection looked at.*

PERSON 10: *This discount doctor is cheap because he doesn't have an actual medical degree or license and doesn't follow any safety standards.*

PERSON 1: *He doesn't have any safety standards, and so he doesn't wash his hands very often.*

PERSON 2: *Since he doesn't wash his hands, he operates on someone else, and my weird infection spreads to that person.*

PERSON 3: *The mixing of my infection and my blood type with this other person's blood type gives this person strange powers.*

PERSON 4: *This person uses those powers to steal money from all of the city banks.*

PEFORMER 5: *The city uses all of its resources to try to stop this super-human before they do any more damage.*

PERSON 6: *With all of the city's resources used, the superhuman moves on to the next city and does the same thing again and again!*

PERSON 7: *Eventually, all of the military comes to try to stop the superhuman but still fails.*

PERSON 8: *With the complete run of the country, the superhuman decides to infect other people to create their own superhuman army.*

PERSON 9: *The superhuman army eventually wipes out all regular humans and then turn on each other.*

PERSON 10: *In one big, epic superhuman battle, only one superhuman remains the survivor.*

PERSON 1: *As the only living being on Earth, this superhuman eventually runs out of ways to get food and parishes.*

EVERYONE: *And the world ends!*

The **goal** here is to heighten one step at a time and build off of what the person before you created and build a story together.

Tips:

- See, it's more fun to start with something boring, such as 'I can't find my shoes,' than starting with something that seems like it will cause a lot of damage. Starting with 'the Prime Minister not being able to find the launch codes' is fine, but it's more fun to start with something uninteresting and building how from that until you get to the destruction of the planet.
- Unlike our actual Earth, once you destroy the world, you can start over with a brand new earth and do the game a few more times.
- Speaking of our real home planet- it's best to use made up situations for each turn, instead of using circumstances that may actually be destroying the world. We want to have fun, not make this warm-up a downer.

Solo Version:

Using the same rules, you can play this game by saying one line at a time and building off of your own ideas. Try not to think ahead or how you will build off something before you say it. We still should be reacting in the moment to something, even if we just said it ourselves.

Awesome Circle (Group)

Skills Used:

* Focus
* Group Chemistry

This is a wonderful game to work on group chemistry and presence, and it works well at the end of a team event. At first, it may seem impossible to accomplish the game, but with enough patience and focus, winning this game always ends in cheers.

How to Play:

1) Everybody stands in a tight circle close enough so each person can put their arms over the shoulders of the person next to them (still a circle, but now a different size one).
2) Next, everyone will be directed, usually by the group leader or someone leading the game who is also in the circle, to look in a few directions together.
3) Everyone looks at the floor, then to their left, then their right, then at the person directly across the circle. If there are two people who could be considered across from them, they can choose one person to be their "directly across the circle" person. Then, finally

ending at the floor again – taking a moment or so between each change of direction. Note: when everyone looks left and right, there should be no eye contact since everyone is looking the same direction.

4) Now that the foundation of the game is set, and everybody is still looking to the floor, the leader counts to three, at which each person in the circle will look either to their left, right, or straight ahead. If they are making eye contact with somebody else, those two people will say, "Awesome!"

5) BUT the **goal** here is that after the count of three, each person will be looking in a different direction, no one will be making eye contact, and there will be an earned moment of silence. This moment of silence signifies that the group is well-connected enough, and they subconsciously know to look into different areas to win the game.

I first came across this game where all the people would yell or scream instead of saying the word *Awesome*. Since that's a bit jarring and feels more negative, this version feels less intense...but you could also replace this word with anything you want. *Gotcha, Howdy, Potato salad...* it doesn't matter. The word is not the goal of the game. Focusing on your group is, and that's pretty genius.

Tips:

– Sometimes, you may reach the moment of silence quickly, and sometimes it takes a very long time. Some people get frustrated when they keep looking at somebody else and feel that they "ruined the game for the group." That's okay though, and it's what happens in the game. Just like how things may seem to 'mess-up' in a meeting, so it may happen here.

– For this warm-up to be successful, everybody in the group has to focus. If after some time people start to get frustrated or start laughing or talking about something else, the group will never reach that end silence. So make sure everybody just takes a breath, focuses and starts again until they reach that moment of silence, because once it has reached, everyone will feel excited they got it and well connected to begin their improv show or class.

Mind Meld - aka Same Word (Group)

Skills Used:

* Focus
* Group Chemistry
* Connecting Ideas

The aim of this group chemistry warm-up is to say the exact same word at the exact same time as someone else. Guess what you're going to do for this warm up? You got it, everybody in a circle!

How to Play:

1) Two people in this circle turn at each other, count out loud to three, and one three, say any word that they want. Now we have two different words.

2) The next pair's job is to think of the single word that connects those previous two words, or is the umbrella word that those two words might fall under.

3) Then they count to three, and say a word simultaneously in hopes that it's the exact same word. If it isn't, then the process will continue until both people land on the same word, without repeating any words that came before it.

A lot of improv exercises and warm-ups are better understood with examples, so how about we give you another example now right here under this sentence I'm writing? Great.

Example:

> PEOPLE 1 & 2: *One.... two... three... Canoe! / Gorilla!*
> (....okay, what one word might connect those two?)
> PEOPLE 2 & 3: *One.... two... three...* Water! / Jungle!
> (...Now these two?)
> PEOPLE 3 & 4: One.... two... three... Island!
> (They did it!)

While the objective is to say the same word as the other person at the same time, it isn't to try to read their lips and say their word with a slight delay, only copying what they are saying. It's for each of you to independently land on the exact same word at the exact same time – hitting that moment of group mind chemistry connection.

The **goal** with this game (that has two names) is again to focus on your fellow improv partner and create more of that group connection. And just like the previous game, it could take a short amount of time or a long time before you finally find success with this warm-up. But once you do, I can almost guarantee that everybody will cheer with their arms in the air. Don't believe me? Try it and find out.

Tips:

— Just like the previous warm-up of Awesome Genius, this one is all about focus. If people are talking, laughing, or getting frustrated, it will never work out. So stay calm and focus on the person you are saying the word with.

- Also, it's very easy to think of a random word by looking up at the ceiling or looking to the side or at the ground, but the point is to get the same word as the other person. So every time you count to three, you have to make direct eye contact with the person you're with. I've done this many times where I didn't even have a word in mind, but by the time I said three, my partner and I somehow ended up saying the same words! So it's really about connecting to the other person.

- While you aren't allowed to repeat any words that have already been said, the word that you want to land on doesn't have to include all of the words previously. It's only the previous two words that you're trying to link up (yikes it would be insane to have to have every word spoken in the entire game connect at once). If you feel like it's been going around for a while and both words are a little too parallel to each other and aren't matching up because you can't repeat something, then it helps for someone just to throw out a completely unrelated word just to get the two threads a little farther apart to then match up again down the line.

- After words have been said that don't match, some people have the urge to then talk about it and say, "I was thinking of this word, but instead, I said this other one, etc. etc." Don't do that. Why? Because you might be saying the word that the next pair can say. So you don't want to lend a hand in any way because that defeats the game's purpose.

Listen to This Moment (Solo)

Skills Used:

* Listening
* Focus

To go along with the Second Circle is another way to bring yourself into the present moment that's very quick and simply, and uses our favorite thing, which is (take a wild guess) listening.

How to Do It:

1) Right now, take this moment and really listen. Hear if you can notice all the sounds in the room. Don't have to label them, don't judge them, you don't even have to question what they are; just hear them. Really try to hear as many different sounds as you can, as if you were listening to a beautiful piece of music.

2) Now try to hear the silences between the sounds. Maybe some sounds come and go, and there's never complete silence, but still, there are at least moments of somewhat-silence between every sound.

3) Next, look around the room and look at your hands. You might notice things that you haven't really noticed before. Right now, you are in the present moment.

Our **goal** here is to open up your listening while really being present and not letting your brain get distracted by all the occurrences that happen around us.

A fun experiment here is to look in the mirror, step away and do this exercise, and then look back in the mirror. If you remain present, you may find out you look a little different than before. Better even!

This is a great exercise you can do any time of the day, whether you are feeling overwhelmed by life or just need a little reset. Improv teaches us to be in the moment and to react from there.

Stretch and Share (Group)

Skills Used:

* Physicality
* Group Connection
* Being Present

Don't you feel like playing a standard silly improv warm-up? Then this one might be right up your alley. It's called "Stretch and Share" because that's literally what you're going to do. You can stand in that group circle if you want, BUT you can also just stand anywhere you want in the space you're in! Finally, a group warm-up not requiring a circle- we did it.

This warm-up expands upon the previously explained "Shake & Stretch" and can be done in a group, instead of by yourself, as that exercise was.

How to Do It:

1) one person will choose a physical stretch that everyone else will do (For example: arms clasped overhead, or bend over, or a squat, or anything else that won't pull a muscle).

2) While everyone in the group is doing that stretch, the person who initiated the stretch will then share some details about their week. It doesn't have to be that exciting, and shouldn't be too long, but just a sentence or two of something they did outside of the group.

3) Then the next person will share a new stretch that everyone will do and a new story about something that happened during their week too.

This might not really seem like an improv warm up, but it is. The **goal** of this section is to be present to your fellow teammates and for yourself to be present in the moment. Simply talking to them and listening while stretching your body and getting a little loosed up has the same effect as any of the previous warm-ups we've said so far. Instead of the overused "How are you?... Good and you?" in which no one really connects or is present, this exercise does that. Plus, we can do with a bit more stretching in our lives.

Questions Only/ABC Lines (Solo or Group)

Skills Used:

* Quick-Thinking
* Building off each other
* Focus

This short form improv game also lends itself to be a good warm up (more about what short form means in a later chapter).

How to Do It:

1) Two people have a normal conversation except- and we're really going to break a big improv rule here- every sentence must be a question.

2) Once someone messes up and says a statement, they're out, and a new person joins, starting a brand new conversation with the person who won that round, again asking only questions

Example:

PERSON ONE: *How do you get to the farmer's market from here?*
PERSON TWO: *You haven't been before?*
PERSON ONE: *Are they even still open?*
PERSON TWO: *What are you looking to get there?*
PERSON ONE: *Do they usually have fresh fruit?*
PERSON TWO: *They do, and they're good.*

(Nope! That's a question and Person One is out.)

A similar version, called ABC Lines, can be done instead, where two people have a conversation going back and forth, except every first letter of each sentence must be the next corresponding letter in the alphabet.

Example:

PERSON ONE: *Great day for a jog today.*
PERSON TWO: *High winds aren't going to stop us.*
PERSON ONE: *I was a little worried you weren't going to show up because of that,*
PERSON TWO: *Jogging is easier when there is wind.*
PERSON ONE: *It kind of sounds like you've done this before.*
PERSON TWO: *Let me tell you about the time I ran a marathon in the windy city of Chicago.*
PERSON ONE: *I've often heard this story but I don't mind hearing it again.*

Just as Questions Only, once someone messes up and says a sentence that begins with the wrong letter, they're out and a new person joins for a brand-new round. The **goal** of both exercises is to keep the conversation going while also playing within the game's parameters.

Solo Version:

To practice this exercise on your own, just go back and forth with yourself, one line at a time, while following the same rules. Every sentence must be a question in response to what you just said, or you can even think of it as talking to yourself out loud, with every sentence following the ABC Lines instructions.

EXERCISE: World's Worst (Solo or Group)

Skills Used:

* Quick-Thinking
* Connecting Ideas
* Comedic Ideas

This popular short-form improv game helps you think of concepts related to various careers. It's a bit like the pun games above, but without the puns – as good or bad as that may be for you.

How to Do It:

1) Create a list of occupations.
2) Then act out a short little vignette of what the World's Worst version of that person doing this particular job would look like. These aren't full scenarios, so it doesn't have to go on too long. It could be a sentence or two just demonstrating whatever the wrong version of someone doing this career might be.
3) Do a few more rounds off of the same occupation before moving onto another on the list and repeating the process.

Example: Race Car Driver

- *I have to drive slowly and follow all traffic laws.*
- *Sorry forgot my glasses. Does that checkered flag so go or stop?*
- *Oh no! I can only make right turns!*

The **goal** here is to get you thinking for humor's sake, and it also helps for initiating ideas you just came up with. Remember, no need to overthink your initiations.

Tips:

- With this, try to think in opposites (*secret to comedy...shhh*) and how a person in this job should NOT act and can go from there. For example: A lawyer should be good at speaking in public, but the world's worst version could be someone who is very bashful (a shy lawyer is very funny!).

Town Hall Meeting (Group)

Skills Used:

* Listening
* Quick-Thinking
* Having Fun
* Public Speaking

This warm-up plays with the worst-case scenario anyone will have to deal with while giving a presentation, as everyone watching the presentation will act as the worst audience members ever. But, it also makes for a very fun exercise.

How to Do It:

1) Choose one or two people as the host speakers of the Town Hall Meeting who will give an improvised presentation on a subject.

2) Someone in the group gives the speakers a subject they probably don't know a lot about (like advanced chemical microbiology), which is more fun than giving them something that will be easy to talk about.

3) The host speakers start giving a talk on the subject to the rest of the group, who will proceed to ask ridiculous questions off on something that was said. Once an audience has a question, they raise their hand, and the hosts call on them to ask the questions. But they shouldn't just be regular questions. They should be really obnoxious questions misinterpreting words and arguing semantics from what the host has spoken.

4) Once asked, the host is *required* to answer it and then continue with their presentation until another question arises.

Example:

> HOST: *Good afternoon, everyone. I'm here to talk about advanced chemical microbiology. I've been studying this for 25 years and...*
>
> (someone raises their hand)
>
> HOST: *Yes, question.*
>
> PERSON IN AUDIENCE: *Hello, yes. You said you've been studying that for 25 years, so when will you take the exam?*
>
> HOST: *There's no exam, but I mean in the study in the field of advanced chemical microbiology.*
>
> (someone raises their hand)
>
> HOST: "Yes?"
>
> PERSON IN AUDIENCE: *Was this field properly mowed, or did the grass get really long?*

See, they aren't asking related questions, but really playing with different meanings of words. You can also think of this as a young child might ask annoying questions to their parents. The **goal** of the host is to answer every question with made up answers and continue their presentation also with made up information since it's a subject they don't know a lot about. The "audience members" goal is to really listen so they can ask frustrating questions to the hosts and keep them on their toes.

Also, you may have noticed that the Host blatantly said "No" and denied the question of there being an exam, which goes against the rule of *Yes, And* in improv. So am I saying the rules don't matter? No (again). The rules of this game are agreed upon by the people playing it (Yes, I will ask annoying questions and they won't fit what information you, as the Host, are asking). So it's still *Yes, And*...and is only acceptable to deny something in this game, not in all of improv.

This is a fun game for either side, and as much as you'd think the Hosts have the harder job, it's pretty easy because you most likely won't be continuing with the presentation but responding to all the questions you'll be getting. Plus, afterward, you'll know that any real –life presentation you'll have to do will never be as bad as this, so that's a confidence builder.

Silent Dialogue (Solo)

Skills Used:

* Quick-Thinking
* Creativity

Don't have access to a group of people to practice your full conversation with all the time? No problem. This exercise is perfect for strengthening that muscle.

How to Do It:

1) Turn on any TV or movie and mute the volume. Like many of the other exercises, don't pick a "good" one but a random one. A program that you are less familiar with is even more helpful here.
2) Start to make up the dialogue between all the characters on screen. Say them out loud and quickly switch to the other person as soon as they begin speaking.

Focus on the **goal** of building good conversations that can continue for a while. It's great to do this for an entire half-hour show as each character will be revisited and can continue the conversation where they left off last time. This is a great way to keep you on your feet, especially because you don't know when the actors' mouths will be moving or when the scene will change. Again, there is no right or wrong answer, so if it doesn't match their real words- totally fine!

Tips:

- It's also fun to do this with another person, and each of you assigns yourselves to one of the characters on screen. If you've ever seen Mystery Science Theater 3000 (or any of its offshoots), they sometimes do the same thing, and it's always a blast!

- Because the actors on screen obviously aren't listening to what you're saying, you will probably be cut off in each sentence you're conveying. That's okay, it just works on keeping you quick on your feet even more.

ACKNOWLEDGEMENTS

I would like to thank, first off, you for reading this book. I worked on it off-and-on for almost a decade, and as I would have more revelations about improv and it's use in everyday life, I'd have to go back and re-write huge sections of the book. It took a lot of time, and editing, and without anyone reading it and gaining useful skills from it, it would all be for nothing. So thanks to you!

Also thanks to every improv, acting, writing, and person-who-inspired-me-to-think teacher I ever studied with. Improv is an on-going and ever-changing art form and without your knowledge and years of experience I would have never been ale to create my own path forward.

With that, thanks to any student who took one of my classes. There's been many of you and by leading you through your own path of creative thinking gave me a better understanding of how humans think and that as different as we all are, we also have a lot in common. And thank you to any group or business who invited my to speak for you – you knew improv had someone thing useful for your team, as much as we could explain what the session would look like, improv always makes every moment unique and memorable.

Thanks to fellow improv teammates whom I've created spontaneous worlds with, some for audiences and some just for ourselves.

Lastly thanks to my friends who have supported my and have watched me on this journey or listened to ideas and thoughts I had from classes. It's true, you really do learn a lot by teaching others.

LEARN MORE

Improv-LA was officially founded by Keith Saltojanes in early 2010 as a place for actors, non-actors, and improvisers to come together to learn and strengthen their skills of creativity, communication, and fearlessness for everyday life. We felt that there was no place in Los Angeles for someone to work on their personal skills and have a creative outlet, without paying thousands of dollars and working their way through a "factory." Thus, Improv-LA is always very affordable and allows its students to explore and workout their creative muscles from the very first moment of class.

The classes are designed to make each student feel confident onstage and off and to let-loose and play in a supportive space. Keith has taken the bare-essentials of all of his experience and training in improvisation, acting, writing, and traveling the world interacting with many cultures and customs and designed a workshop that can be the most beneficial for everyone. Since its start, Keith has brought these workshops to thousands of students from Los Angeles to all around the world and to executives from the biggest companies around (such as Netflix, Amazon, Walt Disney, Anthem Blue Cross, Spotify, Hulu, IBM, Google...) all from a wide variety of backgrounds and walks of life.

If you'd like to learn more from Keith and Improv-LA, see the current available classes. We also have an On-Demand Streaming class for those who are not near Los Angeles!

Visit www.Improv-LA.com for more lessons.